STRATEGIES FOR THE PRACTICE OF INSTITUTIONAL RESEARCH: ONCEPTS, RESOURCES, AND APPLICATIONS

Michael F. Middaugh
Dale W. Trusheim
Karen W. Bauer

Number Nine
Resources in Institutional Research

A JOINT PUBLICATION OF
THE ASSOCIATION FOR INSTITUTIONAL RESEARCH
AND
THE NORTH EAST ASSOCIATION FOR INSTITUTIONAL RESEARCH

TABLE OF CONTENTS

Page

Introduction iii

Chapter 1: Defining the Context for Institutional Research 1
Definition of Institutional Research 1
Selected Institutional Research Measures of Organizational Inputs,
Processes, and Outputs 9

Chapter 2: Identifying Resources for Institutional Research 12
Books, Journals, and Monographs 12
Professional Associations 16
Computing Resources 18
Data Sources 26

Chapter 3: Key Responsibilities of an Institutional Researcher 34
General Data Collection and Reporting 34
Enrollment Management 37
Peer Institutions 41

Chapter 4: Assessment in Institutional Research 44
Introduction to the Concept of Assessment in Institutional Research .. 44
Student Assessment 48
Outcomes Assessment in the I-P-O Model 57
Institution and Personnel Assessment 60

Chapter 5: Finances 64
Ratio Analysis 70
Interinstitutional Financial Data 73
Salary and Compensation Comparisons 76
Salary Equity Analyses 78

Chapter 6: Cost and Productivity Studies 80
General Considerations 82
Specifics on Productivity Analyses 84

Chapter 7: Some Implementation Strategies 91

Appendices 96
  1: Sample AIR Internet Newsletter 96
  2: Standard Production Reports 101
  3: Weekly Admissions Report 105
  4: Weekly Admissions Report With Quality Intervals 108
  5: Cohort Survival Analysis 110
  6: College Selection Survey 112
  7: Career Plans Survey 117
  8: Salaried Staff Interest Survey 120

Index 122

INTRODUCTION

Increasing demands for institutional accountability have created new pressures on colleges and universities to provide information in systematic, timely, and thorough fashion. Reporting requirements associated with State Postsecondary Review Entity (SPRE) mandates, other state-level assessment mandates, directives from regional and professional accrediting bodies, the Federal Student Right to Know Act, and other external forces have converged to raise the institutional research function to new levels of visibility and importance within higher education. This comes at a time when academic and administrative management within the institution is also requiring an increasing volume and variety of information to support policy decisions.

This book aims to provide a conceptual and practical framework for the practice of data/information collection and analysis. While intended to assist practitioners in the field of institutional research, the book was also written with a larger audience in mind. We are confident that this volume will be useful for chief executives, academic and administrative vice presidents, deans and directors, and any other individual interested in the effective collection and use of information to support institutional decision-making and policy development.

One of the challenges in developing this manuscript was to create a publication that would speak to the information and data analysis needs of the diverse array of colleges and universities in higher education – from small, rural community colleges to large, urban research universities. A quick glance at the Association for Institutional Research Directory, for example, shows that the data collection/analysis function at many colleges and universities is performed by an institutional research office staffed with one or more professionals. At other institutions, the function is distributed across offices such as admissions, records and registration, and the like. Moreover, the research and management issues confronting a small, private liberal arts college can be quite different from those at a large, public doctoral university.

Given this broad diversity, we set out to present a framework for institutional research activity which was strategic enough in nature to be applicable to institutions of any size or type. We do not put forth this model with the expectation that every institution will incorporate all aspects of it. Rather, we believe that we have outlined the major components of a comprehensive institutional research operation – whether it is staffed by one person or ten, within a single office or distributed across the organization.

A second major challenge for us was to cover the various topics in sufficient, but not excessive detail. The purpose of this volume is not to provide a detailed, "how to" manual, but to broadly cover strategic approaches to data/information collection and analysis. We think that we have found an appropriate balance in the discussion, but encourage the reader to take advantage of the references cited throughout the text. Of particular value are two other companion volumes in this AIR Monograph Series: *The Primer for Institutional Research* (M. Whitley, J. Porter, and R. Fenske, Eds., 1992), and *Reference Sources: An Annotated Bibliography* (W. Fendley, Jr., and L. Seeloff, Eds., 1993).

This volume is organized as follows. Chapter 1 presents a brief, conceptual framework which centrally places the institutional research function in the higher education environment. We present a fairly simple way to organize a college or university's data/information collection and analysis activities around an input-process-output (I-P-O) model.

Chapter 2 presents many resources which can assist a college or university in implementing a systematic institutional research agenda. For example, we discuss such resources as books and journals, professional organizations, computer software, national information exchanges, electronic telecommunications, and commercially prepared survey instruments, and provide suggestions for their use.

Chapter 3 covers what many view as the more traditional institutional research activities. Because of their centrality to the institution's operation, we have titled this chapter, "Key Components of Institutional Research." Three major concepts in this category include information reporting, enrollment management activity, and comparisons with peer institutions. This chapter discusses some fundamental areas of management information including admissions reporting, official enrollment counts and reports, and attrition and persistence rates. The chapter presents ideas which principally refer to descriptive information which tells the institution precisely where it is at a given point in time.

Chapter 4 presents a wide array of activities which we broadly refer to as "institutional assessment." The chapter discusses areas such as program evaluation, needs assessment, outcomes assessment, and student and employee satisfaction surveys. These assessment activities enable a college or university to monitor the effectiveness of programs and services, and to provide managers with accurate information to support institutional decision-making and policy development.

A fairly new area of institutional research activity is that which supports budget and strategic planning. Chapter 5 describes ways in which the researcher can analyze budget and other financial data to provide management with useful information with respect to revenue and expenditure streams, salary comparisons, and other kinds of interinstitutional benchmarking data. The chapter also describes how financial information can be used within a peer group context to inform institutional decision making.

Chapter 6 discusses the area of faculty and administrative productivity. Strategies for developing productivity measures at the institutional level are described, as are ways of presenting the information for management purposes. Like budget support analysis, this is a relatively new area in institutional research, and is one that is becoming of central importance to campus managers and their external constituencies.

Finally, in Chapter 7, we present several specific strategies for implementing all of the analytical activities described in the preceding chapters. We briefly discuss issues such as coordinating the myriad of data that may be released to the public, writing effective reports, and establishing working relationships with the campus computing center.

This book began in the late 1980s as material prepared by Michael Middaugh for his "Workshop for Newcomers to Institutional Research," presented annually at the Meeting of the North East Association for Institutional Research (NEAIR). An early version of this monograph was written by Middaugh and published under NEAIR sponsorship in 1990. Dale Trusheim and Karen Bauer became involved in the manuscript in 1993 when much of the material was enhanced for presentation at the "Theory and Practice of Institutional Research Workshop" at the 1993 AIR Forum in Chicago, and at the inaugural AIR Institute for the Practice of Institutional Research, held at Northern Kentucky University in Summer of 1993.

We wish to thank and acknowledge the considerable advice we received from the members of the AIR Publications Board, and from several anonymous reviewers in NEAIR. The critical commentary we received from these individuals was extremely helpful as the manuscript went through various drafts. In addition, we are grateful to our colleagues around the country for both their organizational and thematic suggestions about what to include and what to omit from this book. As always, any errors which remain are solely our responsibility.

About the Authors

Michael F. Middaugh, Ed.D., is Director of Institutional Research and Planning at the University of Delaware. Prior to coming to Delaware, he held similar posts at campuses within the SUNY System. A Past President of the North East Association for Institutional Research (NEAIR), he is active on the AIR Professional Development Services Board, and is on the faculty of the AIR Institutes. He has published in the areas of theory and practice of institutional research, and cost containment and faculty productivity. He holds a joint faculty appointment in the University of Delaware's College of Education.

Dale W. Trusheim, Ph.D., is Associate Director of Institutional Research and Planning at the University of Delaware. The author of a book and numerous journal articles in the areas of admissions testing, financial aid research, and enrollment management, he serves on the faculty of the AIR Institute for The Practice of Institutional Research, and has conducted workshops at the Annual Meetings of both AIR and NEAIR. He is former Director of Admissions and Assistant to the President at Washington College in Chestertown, Maryland. He holds a joint faculty appointment in the College of Education at the University of Delaware.

Karen W. Bauer, Ph.D., is Assistant Director of Institutional Research and Planning at the University of Delaware. Before assuming her duties at Delaware, she held positions at the University of Maryland and American College Testing Program, Inc. Active in the leadership of NEAIR and a regular presenter at AIR, NEAIR, and other professional groups, she will join the faculty of the AIR Institute for the Practice of Institutional Research in 1994. She has published in the areas of educational assessment, college student retention, and gender differences. She holds joint faculty appointments in the University of Delaware's Colleges of Arts and Science and Education.

vi

CHAPTER ONE:
DEFINING THE CONTEXT FOR INSTITUTIONAL RESEARCH

What exactly is institutional research and why do we do it? To answer these questions, one must first know a little bit about the information needs of colleges and universities, particularly with respect to policy and decision making.

Institutional research must play a focal role in addressing three questions central to the continued survival of the organization:

1. Where is the organization at this moment? Specifically, what is the "fit" between the college or university's institutional mission and the programs and services which it currently has in place? What is the institution's position within the educational marketplace? Who is the competition and what are they doing? What is the institution doing well at this time? What are the institution's weaknesses and how can they be corrected?

2. Where is the organization going? What do indicators tell us about potential changes in the environment in which we operate? What changes do we need to consider with respect to programs and services currently offered that are: a) consistent with the institutional mission, and b) reflective of changing environmental conditions?

3. How can the organization best arrive at its desired end? What are the alternate courses of action available to the institution in pursuing its objectives? What are the costs associated with implementation of the various alternatives? Can the institution afford to act? Can the institution afford not to act?

Let us use these three general questions to frame the following working definition of institutional research:

Institutional research is the sum total of all activities directed at describing the full spectrum of functions (educational, administrative, and support) occurring within a college or university. Institutional research activities examine those functions in their broadest definitions, and embrace data collection and analytical strategies in support of decision-making at the institution.

An important first step in developing a coherent institutional research program is identification of a conceptual framework for thinking about the research process as it applies to any organization, including colleges and universities. One such framework will be described here, but it certainly is not the only lens for viewing how organizations work. The reader is urged to draw upon his or her training and experience to develop organizing principles and constructs for thinking about organizations and how they operate. Those principles and constructs must be relevant to the researcher, and should provide the general framework for constructing an institutional research program.

One useful way of viewing colleges and universities (or any organization, for that matter), is to think of them as "open systems." From the systems perspective, all organizations are comprised of three central components: inputs, processes, and outputs. In order to function and remain viable, the

Marvin Peterson, a former president of the Association for Institutional Research and an authority on planning and analysis in higher education, has developed, with Linda Vega and Lisa Mets, an annotated bibliography on The Theory and Applications of Institutional Research. It is a highly useful resource, and should be of value to the researcher as he/she refines the conceptual framework for an institutional research program.

Peterson, M.W., Mets, L.A., & Vega, L.R. (1991). Theory and applications of institutional research. In W.R. Fendley & L.T. Seeloff, (Eds.), *Reference Sources: An Annotated Bibliography*. Tallahassee, Florida: Association for Institutional Research.

Additional references that provide good reading on organizational theory include:

Hall, R. H. (1987). *Organizations: Structures, Processes, and Outcomes* (Fourth Edition). Englewood Cliffs, New Jersey: Prentice-Hall, Inc.

Aldrich, Howard E. (1979). *Organizations and Environments*. Englewood Cliffs, New Jersey: Prentice-Hall, Inc.

organization must continuously secure new inputs and process them to generate a "quality" product. Implicit in this cycle of events is an on-going series of transactions with an environment external to the organization. This external environment ultimately supplies the raw materials (inputs) to the organization and serves as the ultimate arbiter as to whether the organizational product has sufficient "quality" to merit consumption.

Figure 1 illustrates the systems concept within the context of higher education. The first major component of the system involves the "inputs" into the higher education enterprise. We require students, faculty, and staff. We need buildings in which to teach and conduct other aspects of educational business. We need money to pay salaries, to buy books and equipment, and to fund other business-related activities. Institutional researchers describe these inputs in a way that answers such fundamental questions as: Who or what are they? How many are there? What do they look like? From which sources do they emanate? Think about the following basic information that is needed about inputs into our colleges and universities:

Students: How many students are enrolled? How many are full-time and how many are part-time? Undergraduate or graduate? What is the overall quality of the student body? What is their general demographic profile?

Faculty: How many full and part-time faculty are employed at the institution? What is the highest earned degree held by each faculty member, and from which granting institution? What is the general demographic profile of the faculty? Is the institution succeeding in attracting the best and brightest young scholars available? At what level of compensation?

Staff: The same general questions asked about faculty also apply to staff. Is the institution attracting the best possible personnel to support the basic educational enterprise?

Facilities: How many buildings on how many acres comprise the campus? What are the age and general condition of the buildings? What is the gross versus net square footage in each building? How efficiently are classrooms and other instructional spaces utilized?

Financial Resources: What proportion of institutional revenues come from tuition and fees? From governmental appropriations? From

3

Figure 1: Conceptual Framework for Analysis of University Functions

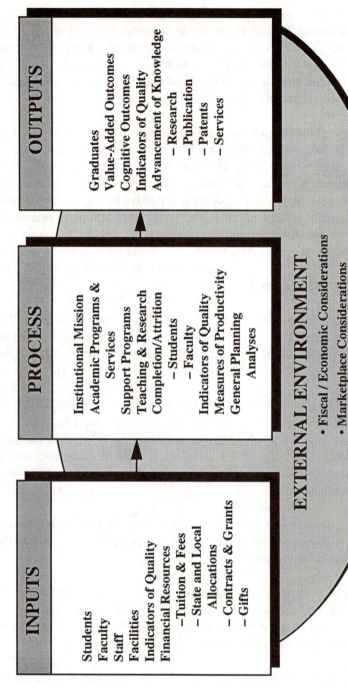

INPUTS

Students
Faculty
Staff
Facilities
Indicators of Quality
Financial Resources
  – Tuition & Fees
  – State and Local
    Allocations
  – Contracts & Grants
  – Gifts

PROCESS

Institutional Mission
Academic Programs &
  Services
Support Programs
Teaching & Research
Completion/Attrition
  – Students
  – Faculty
Indicators of Quality
Measures of Productivity
General Planning
  Analyses

OUTPUTS

Graduates
Value-Added Outcomes
Cognitive Outcomes
Indicators of Quality
Advancement of Knowledge
  – Research
  – Publication
  – Patents
  – Services

EXTERNAL ENVIRONMENT

• Fiscal / Economic Considerations
• Marketplace Considerations
• Government / Regulatory Concerns

contracts and grants? From gifts? From other sources? What is the relative strength of each of these revenue streams?

A similar set of questions can be posed with respect to the "process" component in higher education. The fundamental questions here – and far more difficult to answer – focus on such issues as: What are we doing with the inputs? How are we changing them? Are we doing a good job? Are we doing an efficient job? Consider the following basic process issues:

Institutional Mission: What are the objectives of the educational process at this institution? What is the intended interplay between instruction, research, and public service activity within the context of that mission?

Academic Programs and Services: What degree programs are offered at the institution? What is the depth and breadth of services designed to support those programs (e.g., library, computing, resource centers, advising, counseling, and tutoring services)? How satisfied are the consumers (i.e., students)?

Other Programs and Services: What services are offered to meet the full range of needs of both students and employees (e.g., extracurricular activities, career planning and placement, personal counseling, health/wellness services, mid-career renewal opportunities)? How satisfied are the consumers?

Completion: To what extent do students, faculty, and staff, complete the process for which they were recruited. That is, how many students graduate and how many employees remain until retirement? For what reasons do some students fail to complete?

Quality: Can quality, as it applies to any aspect of the academic enterprise, be measured? If so, where does one begin? Is it possible to obtain comparative measures of quality vis-a-vis other institutions?

Productivity: Do strategies exist for measuring academic and administrative productivity? Are these strategies sensible? What common units of measurement have been defined? Is it possible to distinguish between a "lean" and a "heavy" operation?

Strategic and Budget Planning: How can "process" data be most effectively used in defining institutional direction and in allocating resources to achieve that direction?

Finally, basic questions are posed with respect to the organization's "outputs." What are the tangible products of the processing of organizational inputs? The following issues are ones that concern veteran institutional researchers:

Graduates: How many students graduate from the institution each year, and with which degrees in which disciplines? What is the initial post-graduation employment or graduate school placement? Do graduates feel that their college experience has relevance to post-graduation activity? Do graduates support the institution as alumni?

Personal and Cognitive Skills Outcomes: What behavioral and attitudinal changes can be directly or indirectly attributed to the college or university experience? Can we measure the value "added" by the college experience?" What demonstrable cognitive gains can be measured in those who are "processed" through the college or university experience?

Other Outcomes: To what extent is the college or university contributing to the body of knowledge, as measured in terms of research, publications, patents, and public service?

Simply measuring inputs, process, and outputs is a significant task, in and of itself. The final significant component in this systems approach is to acknowledge that the external organizational environment also has a very profound impact upon the institution's ability to perform its functions. The external environment leads to an additional set of important issues and questions:

Fiscal/Economic Considerations: What is the institution's overall condition with respect to fiscal health? What have the trends been with respect to revenue and expenditure streams for selected institutional functions (i.e., instruction, academic support, student support, financial aid, and facilities maintenance)? How do institutional income and expenditure patterns compare with those of peer institutions? How will external factors such as inflation and the prime interest rate likely affect the institution?

6

Marketplace Considerations: What is the institution's position in the admissions recruiting and faculty recruiting marketplaces? Are enrollment and staffing projections consistent with marketplace considerations? How is the marketplace likely to change during the next 5 to 10 years?

Governmental/Regulatory Considerations: How do governmental regulations, ranging from affirmative action to asbestos abatement affect the organization? How do mandates (outcomes assessment, NCAA compliance, and federal and state reporting requirements) affect operations?

Table 1.1 summarizes many of the types of measures that institutional research officers seek in responding to the foregoing questions raised with respect to inputs, process, and outputs, all within the broader environmental context. The list of measures outlined in Table 1.1 is not exhaustive, but does provide a solid base for assembling information that will begin to describe the various components in the "systems" approach to studying a college or university.

Table 1.1 suggests a number of ways to frame the context and mission of an institutional research office, whether it is a single individual or larger staff. At first glance, it may seem that the task of developing data collection and analytical strategies to address many of the institutional research measures outlined in the table is overwhelming. But, in fact, much of the data are already being collected by institutions for other purposes. What may be required is for the institutional researcher to assemble existing campus data into a usable framework, and then to draw on the ideas presented in Table 1.1 to supplement this context.

In other words, the context for institutional research presented in this chapter argues for a systematic model which involves virtually every major component of an institution of higher education. Of course, the balance of the institutional research effort will vary from institution to institution. Some offices may be more involved with process issues while other offices may do more with budget or financial concerns.

The important point about the I-P-O model is that it presents a useful framework for thinking about institutional research. The institutional researcher should not be continually in a reactive mode – responding to ad hoc requests for data or information only a daily basis. Rather it is helpful to have an on-going, systematic approach to the collection of data and a view for which studies and analyses are most significant.

The remainder of this book describes resources, activities, analyses, and strategies which the institutional researcher can use to develop a program of on-going studies and analyses.

Table 1.1: Selected Institutional Research Measures of Organizational Input, Processes, and Outputs Within the Higher Education Context

I. INPUTS: Fundamental Questions: What are they? How many are there? What do they look like?

SYSTEM COMPONENT   SELECTED MEASURES

Students	Headcount Full/Part Time Status Full Time Equivalency Residence Status Gender Age Transfer / Native	Ethnicity Geographic Origin High School GPA SAT/ACT Scores Financial Aid Major
Faculty and Staff	Headcount Full/Part Time Status Full Time Equivalency Gender Age	Ethnicity Highest Degree Entry Salary Tenure Status
Facilities	Campus Acreage Buildings- Gross Square Footage	Space Inventory Utilization Rates Net Square Footage
Revenues	Tuition and Fees Government Contracts and Grants Gifts	Auxiliaries Endowment Interest Local Taxes

II. PROCESS: Fundamental Questions: What are we doing with inputs? How are we changing them? Are we doing a good job? Are we doing an efficient job?

SYSTEM COMPONENT	SELECTED MEASURES
Institutional Mission, Academic and Support Programs	Degree Program Inventory Course Inventory Support Program Inventory Program Utilization Studies Student Satisfaction Studies Faculty and Staff "Quality of Life" Studies
Completion	Retention/Attrition Analyses Graduation Analyses Faculty Retention Studies Withdrawing/Non-Returning Student Exiting Faculty Studies
Quality	Institutional and Programmatic Accreditations Reputational Ranking of Academic Programs Focus Group / Qualitative
Productivity	Instructional Workload Analyses Faculty Effort Reports Research Grant/Patent Activity Inventory
Strategic/Budget Planning	Trends in Revenues and Expenditures by Financial Ratio Analysis

III. OUTPUTS: Fundamental Questions: What are the tangible products of the processing of organizational inputs?

SYSTEM COMPONENT   SELECTED MEASURES

System Component	Selected Measures
Graduates	Post-Graduation Activity Analysis – Plans of Current Graduates – Career Paths of Older Alumni
Value-Added and Special Skills Outcomes	Student Experiences Analyses
Cognitive Outcomes	Grade Distribution Studies Cognitive Gain Testing Portfolio Analyses
Institutional Outputs	Research Grant Inventory Faculty Publications Analysis Public Service Project Inventory

IV. EXTERNAL ENVIRONMENTAL: Fundamental Question: How are factors external to the institution affecting the conduct of business?

SYSTEM COMPONENT   SELECTED MEASURES

System Component	Selected Measures
Financial Considerations	Consumer Price Index Projections Regional Economic Analyses Educational Price Index Projections
Marketplace	High School Student/Admissions Yield Peer Institutions Comparative Compensation Studies U.S. Census Demographic Projections
Government/Regulatory Concerns	IPEDS Reporting Regional Accreditation Reporting Student-Right-To-Know Asbestos Abatement NCAA Graduation Rates Study Affirmative Action American Disabilities Act

11

CHAPTER TWO:
IDENTIFYING RESOURCES FOR INSTITUTIONAL RESEARCH

A strong institutional research program is aided by knowledge of a broad spectrum of resources, both internal and external to the home institution. For example, various publications, professional organizations, and commercial data collection instruments can supplement in-house databases. Consequently, the purpose of this chapter is to highlight many of the most important resources available to the researcher, and to discuss some of the pros and cons of these possibilities.

I. Books/Journals/Monographs

The following list of books and publications provide excellent introductions to the basic concepts of institutional research. These publications help the researcher to understand the context of higher education and to choose appropriate research methodologies. Because the demands of institutional research vary among institutions, the reader may want to begin with some or all of these publications and then expand the library to meet specific needs.

A. Three volumes describing the rudiments of institutional research are primary resources and essential to every institutional research office:

1. Saupe, J. L. (1990). *The Functions of Institutional Research, 2nd Edition.* Tallahassee, Florida: Association for Institutional Research.

This monograph is a revision of Saupe's 1981 statement of the functions of institutional research. It is a succinct and now classic definition of institutional research – its purpose, place in the higher education organization, responsibilities, and characteristics.

2. Whiteley, M.A., Porter, J. D., & Fenske, R. H. (Eds.). (1992). *The Primer for Institutional Research.* Tallahassee, Florida: Association for Institutional Research.

Whiteley, Porter, and Fenske have assembled a volume of papers from other practitioners in the field who offer helpful tips on data management and on the practice of institutional research in such areas as retention, peer institutions, academic program review, cost analysis, and enrollment management. This volume is an update of the 1987 *A Primer for Institutional Research,* edited by John Muffo and Gerald McLaughlin, and serves as an excellent source of concepts rather than as a "how-to" manual.

3. Presley, J. (Ed.). (1990). *Organizing for Institutional Research* in New Directions in Institutional Research series. San Francisco: Jossey-Bass, Inc.

Presley's volume consists of a description of conceptual contexts for thinking about institutional research, practical strategies for setting up the institutional research office, and suggestions about data collection and analysis processes. This is must reading for new members to the profession.

B. Norris, D.M. & Poulton, N.L. (1987). *A Guide for New Planners.* Ann Arbor, Michigan: Society for College and University Planning.

Designed to introduce college administrators to the central issues in planning processes within higher education, the value of this book to the institutional researcher is its definition of areas where quantitative analysis supports institutional planning.

C. Russell, A. B., & Rodriquez, E. M. (Eds.). (June, 1993). *Compendium of National Data Sources on Higher Education.* Denver: State Higher Education Executive Officers.

State Higher Education Executive Officers (SHEEO) has published a valuable resource book which provides information about the variety of higher education data sources that are available. This volume contains information on the major national data sources related to higher education, including "surveys and databases, reports, statistical digests and other means of making data available" (*Compendium,* p. xiii). If institutional researchers need information about virtually any source for data about higher education, this volume will have a description of the source and how to contact someone to obtain these data.

D. The National Center for Higher Education Management Systems (NCHEMS) produces a number of useful publications which may be especially helpful to newer institutional researchers:

1. *Executive Overview Series.* NCHEMS issued a series of monographs in the early 1980s which are especially relevant for the institutional researcher:

• Jones, D.P. (1982). *Data and Information for Executive Decisions in Higher Education.*

• Barak, R.J. (1982). *Program Review in Higher Education: Within and Without.*

• Chaffee, E.E. (1982). *Rational Decision Making in Higher Education.*

• Ewell, P.T. (1983). *How to Acquire and Use Student-Outcomes Information.*

• Brinkman, P. & Krakower, J. (1983). *Comparative Data in Higher Education.*

These volumes discuss data collection, analysis, and policy issues from the perspective of senior administrators. The monographs provide useful insights into the types of information that presidents and vice presidents request, as well as the ways in which they are likely to use that information in making decisions.

Note that the identification and use of peer comparison-groups is a common task for institutional researchers and readers are encouraged to consult the Brinkman and Krakower manuscript.

2. Christal, M.E. & Jones, D.P. (1983). *A Common Language for Post Secondary Accreditation: Categories and Definitions for Data Collection.*

Christal and Jones present a valuable reference for a common analytical language among institutional researchers. This volume clearly details a comprehensive listing of the data elements that must be collected to describe the full range of activities within a higher education institution. They also provide common definitions for analyzing those data elements in such a way to permit inter-institutional comparison. For example, full time equivalent students and staff, credit hours, contact hours, fiscal and physical space measures should all be developed from a common set of definitions to make valid comparisons with peer institutions.

The NCHEMS references cited above, as well as a full catalog of additional publications, can be obtained from the National Center for Higher Education Management Systems, P.O. Drawer P, Boulder, Colorado 90302.

E. Kells, H.R. (1987). *Self-Study Processes: A Guide for Postsecondary Institutions*. Washington, D.C.: American Council on Education.

Kells is an authority on institutional self study processes, and has developed this comprehensive handbook to guide colleges and universities through regional accreditation and/or professional program accreditation. The handbook clearly defines the data needs in a self-study and suggests ways in which the institutional researcher can establish a central role in that process.

F. The following journals and monograph series have proven especially helpful to institutional researchers, both newcomers and experienced practitioners:

1. *Research in Higher Education*. This is the scholarly journal of the Association for Institutional Research and provides a forum for publishing results of important quantitative studies or conceptual papers by leading practitioners in the field. Major researchers use this journal to share concepts, methodologies, and the analytical results of studies. The methodologies and approaches to answering questions about higher education are frequently helpful to researchers contemplating similar analyses at their home institutions. *Research in Higher Education* is of central importance for keeping abreast of the field.

2. *New Directions for Institutional Research*. This is an ongoing series of monographs published by the Association for Institutional Research in cooperation with Jossey-Bass Publishers. Each volume is organized around a central theme, such as admissions marketing, retention, academic planning and evaluation, cost studies, using national databases, and Total Quality Management (TQM). Four volumes are published annually, each with a different editor, containing a collection of contributed papers from leading practitioners in the field.

3. *Journal of Higher Education*. Published by the American Association for Higher Education, this journal provides scholarly treatment of contemporary issues in higher education. Scanning the environmental context in which postsecondary institutions operate is vital and this journal is an excellent means of doing so.

4. ASHE/ERIC Higher Education Reports. Published jointly by the Association for the Study of Higher Education and ERIC Clearinghouse, each volume in the series examines research that has been completed on a contemporary issue in higher education. The volumes provide an opportunity to think in depth about such areas as faculty burn-out, student stress syndrome, federal and state obligations to higher education, academic program review, or student financial aid. Ideas for in-house research projects often originate from this series of monographs.

5. AIR Professional File. Each issue of the AIR Professional File deals with a specific theme designed to augment the professional knowledge of members of the Association for Institutional Research. Up to four issues a year are sent to members of the Association. A representative sample of recent topics include electronic mail, conducting employer surveys, and strategic planning and organizational change.

6. *The Chronicle of Higher Education*. The trade newspaper, the *Chronicle of Higher Education*, is an indispensable source of information on federal and state legislation. In addition, the "Fact File" is a fingertip source of normative data for inter-institutional and interstate comparisons of faculty and staff salaries, student achievement test scores, student migration patterns, educational philanthropy, etc.

II. Professional Associations

Perhaps the most valuable resources available to us in institutional research are our colleagues. Our profession rests on a foundation of people who share knowledge, concepts, ideas, methodologies, and study results. The following professional associations are especially useful:

1. Association for Institutional Research (AIR). AIR is the national organization for institutional researchers. Its Annual Forum, held in late spring, is an opportunity to meet colleagues from across the country, as well as with leading scholars in various areas of higher education research. The Forum's contributed papers reflect both theory and practical advice on conducting institutional research. Practical strategies for institutional research are also available through a series of round table discussions organized around current research topics, and held throughout the Forum.

The AIR Forum also provides workshops for newcomers and experienced institutional researchers. Workshops offered at recent meetings include such important areas as effective reporting, outcomes assessment, Total Quality Management, survey research, and introductory statistics. In addition to workshops and round table discussions, numerous special interest groups also meet at the national level.

In addition, AIR provides the opportunity to expand the network of contacts among institutional researchers from a regional to a national base. Through contacts made at professional meetings, a colleague with an answer to that difficult problem is only a phone call or electronic mail message away. AIR can be contacted by writing to: AIR Secretary, 314 Stone Building, Florida State University, Tallahassee, Florida 32306.

2. Regional/State Associations. Regional institutional research associations such as North East AIR, Southern AIR, Midwest AIR, Rocky Mountain AIR, California AIR, and state associations such as those in Connecticut, California, and New Hampshire, provide forums for exploring higher education issues on a more local level. The annual regional AIR meetings tend to be more pragmatic, with a "nuts and bolts" approach to problem solving. Similar to the national AIR, the annual meetings also offer numerous workshops where both newcomers and experienced researchers can learn new skills or discuss new approaches to old problems. A full listing of regional associations is available from the Association for Institutional Research (address above).

As well, many of the regional associations offer monographs on specific institutional research topics, written by members of the regional association. The monographs are pragmatic rather than theoretical in orientation; the emphasis is clearly on a "how to" methodology. Another significant benefit of the regional associations is that they allow the institutional researcher to establish a local network of institutional research professionals.

3. Society for College and University Planning (SCUP). SCUP brings together institutional personnel involved in planning. In addition to institutional research persons, who make up a significant portion of the membership, academic vice presidents, deans, administrative vice presidents, budget personnel, and facilities personnel are all represented among the membership. SCUP focuses on planning issues ranging from enrollment and academic planning to budget and facilities planning. Institutional researchers will find SCUP meetings, and its journal, *Planning*, particularly useful in defining the quantitative needs of personnel typically associated with campus planning

processes. SCUP can be contacted by writing: SCUP Secretary, 2026M School of Education Building, University of Michigan, Ann Arbor, Michigan 48109.

4. National Center for Higher Education Management Systems (NCHEMS). In addition to the excellent publications described earlier in this chapter, NCHEMS provides a number of professional seminars at locations throughout the country on such topics as assessing student outcomes, linking planning and budgeting, and cost analysis in higher education. The full range of NCHEMS services, as well as a discussion of membership benefits, can be obtained by writing: NCHEMS, P.O. Drawer P, Boulder, Colorado 90302.

5. American Association for Higher Education (AAHE). In addition to publishing *The Journal of Higher Education*, AAHE is the prime moving force in the country in the area of assessment. AAHE meetings and workshops provide scholars, practitioners, central administrators, and legislators an occasion to discuss the latest assessment research. AAHE can be contacted by writing: AAHE Secretary, One Dupont Circle NW, Suite 600, Washington D.C. 20036.

6. Association for the Study of Higher Education (ASHE). ASHE's Annual Meeting is an opportunity for institutional researchers and faculty scholars to discuss central issues in research in higher education. ASHE is especially useful in framing studies relative to faculty activity, workload issues, the instructional process, and general assessment considerations. ASHE can be contacted by writing: ASHE Secretary, One Dupont Circle NW, Suite 630, Washington, D.C. 20036.

III. Computing Resources

Choosing the best technology for administrative tasks, word processing, and data analysis can be a confusing and frustrating process. When many veteran institutional researchers first entered the profession, for example, virtually all computerized data analyses were run on a mainframe computer, with connection established directly via a "dumb" terminal or a microcomputer with some early telecommunication software. Today institutional researchers are dealing with servers, ethernet, token rings, workstations, local area networks, and a dizzying array of statistical software, word processing and graphics packages, spreadsheets, desktop publishing software, and CD-ROM possibilities. The purpose of this section is not to recommend specific products, but rather to discuss many of the options and resources available to institutional researchers in the selection of computer tools.

A. Mainframe Computers, Workstations, and Microcomputers

In the majority of cases, institutional researchers must simply adapt to the computing environment (mainframe and databases) that is already in place at a college or university. And, a great deal of the data needed to conduct a solid, on-going program of institutional research already exists in most institutions of higher education. Students apply for admission, enroll, register for courses, receive grades, and eventually leave, either through graduation or attrition. Faculty and staff are recruited and placed on salary. Goods are purchased and bills are paid. All of these transactions exist in recorded form somewhere in the institution, in most instances in computerized format. A mainframe computer(s) is typically where institutional data (e.g., Admissions, Financial Aid, Student Records, Course Registration, Accounts Receivable, Personnel, Alumni databases) reside, and is reserved principally for file storage, programming tasks, large "number crunching" and "standard" reporting tasks (e.g., federal IPEDS reports), and tape manipulation.

One of the most important jobs of the institutional researcher is to become familiar with the various campus databases and their associated data element dictionaries. The goal is to determine which data already reside at the institution. A meeting with the Director of the Computer Center, with an eye toward obtaining relevant data element dictionaries, is a necessity. For example, which specific data elements exist in the Admissions Data Base, the Student Records System, the Course Registration File, the Financial Aid File, the Personnel File, or the Budget File? The answer to that question can be a pleasant surprise although it is sometimes difficult to obtain data in a format that permits *easy* analysis.

Most colleges and universities in the United States participate annually in the Integrated Postsecondary Education Data System (IPEDS) reporting system. The IPEDS system requires an annual fall semester report of student enrollments, personnel staffing, academic support, and fiscal data. These data are reported by a number of sub-variables, e.g., gender and ethnicity of students, faculty, and staff. In order to complete IPEDS reports, many institutions have computerized reporting systems which are veritable gold mines to institutional researchers.

The IPEDS reporting coordinator is usually located in the Office of Institutional Research, the Registrar's Office, or the Academic Vice President's Office. A thorough examination of the IPEDS reporting documents, whether computerized or hard copy, will provide a solid base for reviewing the institution's total management information system, and assessing which data elements are readily available to support local institutional research objectives.

Desktop computers today possess many of the capabilities that were offered only by large mainframe machines as recently as five years ago. Most of the computing requirements in a contemporary institutional research office can now be handled on a desktop microcomputer, assuming of course, that the desktop machine has the capability to contact institutional mainframes or workstations.

For example, the desktop microcomputer can be used for sophisticated enrollment projections, fiscal analyses, and other statistical analyses if the number of cases and variables in the analysis are manageable. "Manageability" simply refers to the capacity, as defined by staff time and computer disk space, to collect, transfer, download, and/or enter data into the software package being used in the analysis. This is a judgment call on the part of the researcher; experience shows that many projects are appropriate for the microcomputer's capabilities.

As well, software exists that enables the desktop microcomputer to "emulate" a mainframe terminal, thus allowing the researcher to select specific data elements and cases from large mainframe databases, develop a smaller data subset, and download that subset to the desktop microcomputer's disk for analysis. This downloading capability is particularly useful for importing data into spreadsheet or statistical software packages such as Lotus 1-2-3, Excel, SAS PC, or SPSS PC.

Finally, more and more large-scale data sets are becoming available via CD-ROM technology. For example, some Census data, Current Population Survey data, Regional Economic Information System (REIS) and USA Counties data are now available via CD-ROM. The advantages of the CD-ROM approach is that all information pertaining to the data is contained on a single CD. Researchers have the codebook and all raw data at their fingertips.

B. Software

Because microcomputers are such an integral part of the operation of most offices and can provide some of the analytical firepower required by institutional research offices, this discussion of software centers on options available for enhancing the microcomputer's capabilities. In addition to the software options discussed below, the reader is encouraged to pursue additional possibilities in computer magazines such as *PC, PC Week, Personal Computing, MacWorld,* and *MacUser.*

1. Electronic spreadsheets: As the name implies, the electronic spreadsheet is a vehicle for arraying data on a computer screen and for developing mathematical formulas to describe the relationships among the data cells on the spreadsheet. Originally used for financial analyses, the electronic spreadsheet has gained favor among institutional researchers as an effective tool for performing other types of studies as well. Spreadsheets lend themselves particularly well to simple tasks such as sorting a short list of competitor institutions and their associated tuition or faculty salary data. Contemporary spreadsheet packages are also able to handle much more complicated tasks such as institutional enrollment projection models as well as tuition or other revenue forecasting models.

The Lotus and Microsoft Corporations are the major forces in the electronic spreadsheet market. Whether the researcher chooses Lotus 1-2-3 or Microsoft Excel, the quality and support of these spreadsheets is difficult to surpass. Each comes with a self-paced tutorial, and many colleges and universities offer in-house training on advanced use of electronic spreadsheets. The Lotus and Microsoft products are also considerably augmented with graphing, word processing, and basic statistical capabilities. Moreover, the products can be used in conjunction with a wide range of other statistical and word processing software packages.

2. Statistical software packages: While a multitude of software packages enable sophisticated, high powered statistical treatment of data, most institutional researchers use either the Statistical Package for the Social Sciences (SPSS) or Statistical Analysis Software (SAS). Both SPSS and SAS are available in mainframe and microcomputer versions. Each is thoroughly documented and comes with full support and training opportunities. Since many colleges and universities have both software packages on-line, the choice will likely come down to the package with which the researcher is most familiar.

Each statistical package allows the reader to easily define the location of variables in a dataset, conduct any necessary data transformations, weightings, or other manipulations of the data file. Descriptive statistics and simple frequency distributions provide base line information on data sets. As well, crosstabulations and measures of association, tests for differences between means, parametric and nonparametric correlational measures, analysis of variance, multiple regression, logistic regression, factor analysis, and many other statistical procedures are available from both packages. Both SPSS and

21

SAS also provide add-on software components such as graphs and report-ready tables. Note that many researchers, however, opt to execute graphs and charts from a separate spreadsheet-based graphics package, or from a graphics package on a desktop computer.

Regardless of whether the software package selected is SPSS, SAS, or one from another vendor, it should have the capability to do both base line descriptive statistics as well as more complex multivariate procedures. Equally important, the package should enable the definition and manipulation of data and variables. Because they capture all of these capabilities in a single package, and do so in a relatively user-friendly manner designed for the non-programmer, SPSS and SAS are the leaders in the field.

3. Word Processing and Desktop Publishing: Most institutional researchers write reports and conduct data analyses for senior campus administrators. These administrators are more likely to read analytical reports and institutional studies that are professionally prepared and visually attractive.

Word processing has evolved far beyond computerized typing capabilities. A capable word processing software package combined with a high quality laser printer results in typeset-quality publishing. An abundance of word processing software for both IBM and IBM-compatible or Macintosh computers provides many choices for the researcher. Among the leaders in word processing are WordPerfect and Microsoft Word (available for both IBM and Macintosh computers). Computer magazines frequently review these and many other software packages for the prospective buyer, as well as detailing the full range of capabilities of word processing. Highly varied font selection, bold print and italics, color graphics, basic arithmetic functions, and even clip art for added illustration possibilities, are commercially available at modest cost.

Research offices which conduct survey research should also consider investing in desktop publishing hardware and software. A high quality laser printer is, of course, a prerequisite. Laser printers which offer as high as 600 dpi output are now very affordable. Page layout programs such as Aldus Pagemaker or QuarkXPress make locally-designed surveys appear professionally type set, although in many instances, the current versions of Microsoft Word or WordPerfect may well suffice.

Many colleges and universities have microcomputer resource consultants which advise faculty, students, and staff about the pros and cons of each package. Consult with these or other knowledgeable computer users before making final purchase decisions.

4. Graphics and Presentation Software: The tremendous growth in software for the personal computing field has led to additional opportunities for institutional researchers. In the future, the well-equipped institutional research office should include graphics packages, presentation software, and perhaps even multimedia applications. For example, the incorporation of charts and graphs into reports can significantly enhance their readability. As well, ink jet color printers are now very affordable and make it easy to generate color charts and color overhead transparencies. Some of the stand-alone charting software seen frequently on DOS-based machines is Harvard Graphics, Freelance, or CorelDraw. Comparable packages used on Macintosh computers include both DeltaGraph Professional and CA-Cricket Graph.

The recent advent of powerful portable computers and current versions of presentation software have also expanded the world of display technology. The two software packages that now lead the field in presentation software are Persuasion by Aldus and PowerPoint by Microsoft Corporation. Institutional researchers may use these packages to create color overhead transparencies, 35 mm slides, or to run computer generated slide shows replete with any number of between-slide transition effects. Prior to portable computers, one had to carry a desktop computer to the meeting. With the availability of powerful, small, portable computers, however, it is now possible to quickly set up a computer-generated slide show for presentation to internal or external audiences. Hardware requirements are simply the notebook computer, a color LCD panel, and a powerful projector (e.g., DuKane).

C. Electronic Communication

Since the late 1980s, electronic mail and computer networking have tremendously expanded the opportunities available to faculty and administrators in higher education. For example, an institutional researcher can conduct brief, e-mail surveys in various ways to obtain within one day, feedback from other researchers or individuals connected to the network. Institutional researchers can share actual data files, input programs, and texts of articles that might be co-authored. It is also possible to connect to computers at remote locations to obtain archived information, computer files or even specific software. Further, an institutional researcher can "subscribe" to various electronic newsletters, bulletin boards, or discussion lists to stay up-to-date on a daily basis with topics of interest.

There are many significant, new possibilities with respect to electronic communication and the institutional researcher. Newcomers to institutional researcher should become familiar with the existing status of e-mail at their institution.

1. Internal Electronic Mail. Many schools now utilize internal electronic mail that, in many cases, has effectively replaced phone and memorandum communication. For example, faculty, professional staff, students, and many support staff personnel have e-mail addresses. It is possible to send memos, notes, reminders, queries, and other information directly to a colleague's mail address at a microcomputer on that individual's desk. Unless the computer network crashes, e-mail reaches the addressee faster than phone messages or regular campus mail. The resulting improvement in the efficiency and speed of communication is valuable.

Another possible internal use of electronic mail is to communicate "run" requests for certain jobs that are programmed to run on the mainframe. At the beginning of every term, many schools need to generate counts of the number of students who are officially enrolled. Before electronic mail, this was usually accomplished by submitting a paper request to the computing center. With an electronic submission, the request is both filed in the computer and transported almost instantly to the computing center where the job can be promptly scheduled. Future requests for the same information but new terms can be easily retrieved from the computer and submitted.

2. External Electronic Mail. Many colleges and universities now offer access to electronic networks to faculty, administrators, and students. The two principal networks available to individuals in academic settings are the Internet and Bitnet. The Internet has become the electronic network utilized most frequently by higher education institutions, business, and the federal government, and has seen tremendous growth in the last three years. As more and more institutions join the Internet, Bitnet will probably become part of the larger Internet. In addition, there are a great many other commercial electronic networks available (e.g., CompuServe, Prodigy, and America Online), but access to these networks is accompanied by monthly user charges. Institutions and businesses do pay fees to use the Internet, but these costs are not typically charged back to individual units within the organization.

If an institution offers access to either the Internet or Bitnet, it will be well worth the institutional researcher's time to master the syntax necessary to use these networks. If the institution does not have access, it would be worthwhile exploring methods of connecting such as obtaining a "guest" account at a nearby college or university.

Access to the Internet enables the researcher to accomplish a variety of tasks. One advantage is that the institutional researcher can subscribe to various electronic newsletters and discussion lists. Appendix 1 is a printed copy of a recent Association for Institutional Research (AIR) Newsletter. Subscription to the Electronic AIR will provide the user with approximately one newsletter per month. The newsletter contains a variety of useful information, such as general news; requests for advice or assistance on institutional research projects; notices about future developments and issues in higher education; news about member activities; and job announcements.

Discussion lists are somewhat different from the newsletter shown in Appendix 1. Literally hundreds of discussion lists are available through the Internet or Bitnet. It is possible to obtain a List of Lists, which is simply the name and location on the Internet for most of the discussion lists that are currently active. These lists include a tremendously broad range of topics: total quality management, executive information and decision support systems, outcomes assessment, the PASCAL programming language, statistics, supercomputers, qualitative research, or the latest Macintosh and IBM operating systems. There are SPSS and SAS discussion lists, both of which are regularly monitored by the statistical support staff at those companies. If a researcher has a question about the LOOP procedure in SPSS, it is possible to submit a question to the list, and have it responded to by other SPSS users who subscribe to the list, or possibly by SPSS technical support.

Access to these international electronic networks also permits the institutional researcher to communicate with mainframe computers at other universities. In other words, it is a straightforward task to use the Internet to log on to a computer at Stanford or the University of Minnesota to look up publicly available data on their mainframes. Such institutionally-specific data may include institutional fact books or other information about the school.

Both Bitnet and Internet allow one to *retrieve* data or text files, and even actual applications for one's desktop computer. There is now a wide variety of software available for file retrieval or file searching. Some of the more well-known applications are Gopher, Fetch, and Archei. The United States Department of Education and the Office of Educational Research and Improvement offer on-line announcements, bulletins, and press releases. The full text and executive summaries of official government studies, reports, and policy analyses are accessible on-line.

The Internet provides literally boundless resources. In addition to institutional information, Census data and other national databases, researchers can also retrieve computer files and applications. For example, many Macintosh files (e.g., shareware, utilities, movies, and sounds) are archived at Stanford University. Using a Macintosh file transfer protocol such as Fetch, it is possible to log on to the Stanford mainframe and retrieve the desired computer file or program. Once the file resides on the mainframe, it then takes a second step to "download" the file from the mainframe to a desktop computer.

The correct procedures to utilize the Internet varies depending upon the mainframe computer and operating environment at individual institutions. The thing to do is to consult with your local computer services department for information about the network, correct syntax, and even e-mail protocol.

Good, recent references about the Internet are:

Krol, E. (1992). *The Whole Internet: User's Guide and Catalog*. Sebastopol, California: O'Reilly and Associates.

Mrine, A., Kirkpatrick, S., Neou, V., and Ward, C. (1993). *Internet: Getting Started*. Englewood Cliffs, New Jersey: PTR Prentice Hall.

Two earlier, but helpful volumes about electronic mail and how they are useful to the institutional research profession include:

Dunn, J.A. (1989). Electronic media and information sharing, in *Enhancing Information Use in Decision Making* (Peter Ewell, Ed.), *New Directions for Institutional Research, No. 64*, San Francisco: Jossey-Bass, Inc.

Updegrove, D.A., Muffo, J.A., & Dunn, J.A. (1990). Electronic mail and networks: New tools for institutional research and university planning. Tallahassee, Florida: AIR Professional File, No. 34.

IV. Data Sources

Occasionally, it is necessary to collect data from sources other than the institution's computerized files. These externally collected data are generally acquired in one of two ways: 1) in the form of a professionally prepared data set, or 2) through data collection activity (survey, interview, etc.), frequently directed by the Office of Institutional Research.

A. External Data Sources

A. Professionally Prepared Data Sets. Entrepreneurs abound who are ready to provide institutional researchers with data sets addressing any number of institutional variables in virtually any computer-compatible format. A trip to the vendors' corner at any professional meeting will quickly confirm this observation. Before purchasing a data set, try to find other institutional researchers who have used the products and who might be able to indicate general satisfaction or problems.

Four major sources of prepared data sets have proven consistently reliable over time:

1. Integrated Postsecondary Education Data System (IPEDS). The IPEDS system has been described above. Some institutional researchers are unaware that the data reported by colleges and universities is in the public domain. Each year, IPEDS data for a given reporting year (generally 18 to 24 months behind the current year) becomes available on computer tape. Separate tapes are produced for the major IPEDS reporting categories: students, personnel, and fiscal data. The tapes are accompanied by file layouts, and can be analyzed using many statistical software packages. Thus, comparison is possible of institutional data for that reporting category with data from any other institution in the nation participating in the IPEDS program which, as noted earlier, is the vast majority of postsecondary institutions.

A very new way to obtain IPEDS information is now offered in The National Cooperative Data Share™ (NCDS). NCDS is a campus-to-campus public service program maintained by John Minter Associates and made available on the Internet through the University of Virginia Social Science Data Center. "The mission of NCDS is to make current campus survey statistics available as quickly as possible for institutional comparison, planning, and budgeting" (NCDS online documentation).

Colleges and universities input their IPEDS statistics on a floppy disk with software developed by Minter Associates. The disk is then mailed to Minter and the data are loaded into NCDS. Once the institution has therefore joined the NCDS consortium, the school is able to get into the University of

Virginia gopher location and view or download IPEDS data for any other institution which has also provided these data.

The extremely quick turnaround time of this new service is what is valuable. Rather than wait over a year for the tapes to become available, researchers can see Fall 1993 IPEDS statistics for other institutions as early as January, 1994. Also, the entire service is free. The only cost to the institution is data entry time to put the IPEDS statistics on the disk.

There is a third alternative to purchasing the tape. Each state has an IPEDS coordinator, usually within the State Department of Higher Education. The State IPEDS Coordinator receives a complimentary set of tapes which can be made available to participating institutions. The National Center for Educational Statistics, within the U.S. Department of Education, is the coordinating agency for IPEDS. Their address is: 555 New Jersey Avenue NW, Washington, DC 20208.

2. The College Board Annual Survey of Colleges. The College Entrance Examination Board (CEEB) collects from all colleges and universities detailed institutional characteristics such as headcounts by gender, student level, full/part time attendance status, ethnicity, tuition charges, financial aid data, degree programs offered, program accreditations, support program data, and freshman admissions data. This information is collected for publication in the College Boards' annual *Handbook*. However, the College Board also makes this entire data set available on disk or tape, with supporting documentation for statistical software packages. The cost of a single tape is approximately $500. If the institutional researcher wants to maintain a comprehensive profile of competitor institutions, this data file is a worthwhile purchase every few years. Information about this service can be obtained by contacting the College Board, 45 Columbus Avenue, New York City, New York 10023.

3. National Data Service for Higher Education. John Minter and his associates have identified typical inter-institutional comparisons using IPEDS data and the College Board Annual Survey of Colleges. They have separated those comparisons into a series of analyses, generally over a multi-year time period, grouped according to Carnegie institution type, (e.g., research and doctoral universities, comprehensive colleges and universities, liberal arts colleges I, and liberal arts colleges II). Each classification type is further separated by public or independent status. The analyses cover financial statistics, enrollment statistics, library statistics, institutional characteristics, compensation statistics, degrees awarded, academic and support programs, and

admissions statistics, among others. The data are available in either hard copy or diskette.

Minter's data sets save time in developing analytical computer programs, and have the distinct advantage of providing trend data in a single source document at an attractive price. The major disadvantage, however, comes when comparing the institutional researcher's institution to more than one Carnegie institutional type, e.g., to both public and private doctoral research universities. At the point when multiple volumes or diskettes have to be purchased, the cost and time spent on the analysis becomes more extensive. Also, in the instance of fiscal analyses, the user will have to become familiar with the principles of ratio analysis.

Minter is continually refining his data services. Recent additions include the electronic availability of IPEDS data through the National Cooperative Data Share cited above, and a service called "ReadyStats" which provides various educational statistics and comparative data on an electronic bulletin board. A complete catalog of Minter data sets and services can be obtained by writing to: National Data Service for Higher Education, 2400 Central Avenue B-2, Boulder, Colorado 80301.

4. Data Sharing Consortia. Several formal data sharing consortia are currently operating in higher education. Some of the largest organizations of this type are the Higher Education Data Sharing Consortium (HEDS), the Public Universities Data Exchange (The Exchange), the Association of American Universities (AAU), and the Southern University Group (SUG).   These organizations of colleges and universities are committed to sharing data from annual national data collections (e.g., IPEDS Surveys, AAUP Survey of Faculty Salaries, NCAA Graduation rates), as well as special studies that may be commissioned by member institutions.

The great value of this consortia approach is that it permits a more timely sharing of important data as opposed to waiting for public release of these documents. As well, the consortia allow the membership to conduct studies of more specific, local issues. Each of these consortia meet regularly as Special Interest Groups during the Association for Institutional Research Annual Forums. To obtain information about these groups, researchers can attend the Annual Forum, or simply request information from the national Association for the correct contact person at the data sharing consortium.

B. Commercial Surveys

On those occasions when institutional researchers need data not commercially available they must collect it themselves. Generally, the primary vehicle for such quantitative data collections is a survey. When faced with a data collection project that requires a survey instrument, two courses of action are available: purchase a commercially prepared instrument or develop a questionnaire locally.

Commercially prepared survey instruments are abundant. Depending upon the specific research need, it is recommended that the two companies listed below be contacted as a starting point. Each specializes in admissions marketing surveys, student satisfaction surveys, withdrawing or non-returning student surveys, alumni surveys, and others. Moreover, each has instruments to measure cognitive learning gains. One principal advantage of using a national survey is that normative data by institution type is available; hence a single institution can be compared to national averages. In some cases, specific subgroup norms are also available. Full catalogs and samples of commercial instruments are available from each:

Educational Testing Service
Princeton, New Jersey 08541
Telephone: 609-734-1105

American College Testing Program
P.O. Box 168
Iowa City, Iowa 52243
Telephone: 319-337-1000

Note also that frequently, these commercially-prepared instruments can be evaluated at professional meetings. In many cases, papers will be presented that use results obtained from the surveys so the researcher may assess the practical usefulness of these instruments.

C. Locally Prepared Surveys

Sometimes the development of a locally-prepared survey is the best alternative for obtaining the needed information. Some questions may be quite specific to an institution, and national instruments may be simply unavailable. For example, some higher education institutions have studied the use and satisfaction of students or the faculty with the campus computing environment. Or perhaps an institution is interested in assessing a specific aspect of students' social life such as alcohol use or acquaintance rape. Chances are that nationally-normative instruments will not be available with the needed level of detail. In these cases, therefore, a locally developed survey can be developed to provide the desired information. If an institutional researcher embarks on this path, the following suggestions may be helpful:

1. Obtain a copy of an excellent monograph, *Questionnaire Survey Research: What Works*, by Linda A. Suskie (Tallahassee, FL: Association for Institutional Research, 1992). This book contains a wealth of practical tips on developing a good instrument, enhancing return rates, and analyzing data. Examples of good instruments are accompanied by equally useful examples of bad instruments. Copies of the monograph can be obtained by writing to: Association for Institutional Research, 314 Stone Building, Florida State University, Tallahassee, FL, 32306.

2. Examine electronic discussion lists which offer critiques of, or which serve as clearinghouses for survey instruments. Occasionally, the RESEARCH and ASSESSMENT discussion lists offer critiques of relevant information. Also, the electronic AIR (discussed above) is a forum where researchers can request that other survey researchers share copies of surveys that have been employed at local levels. Presently, there is a discussion underway on an assessment electronic list about beginning a clearinghouse for student life/development survey instruments.

3. Be sure to utilize the campus library and scholarly journals to obtain information about the intended survey topic. If, for example, you have been asked to develop a survey about alumni satisfaction, and you are not familiar with this topic, obtain information about the theory and practice of alumni satisfaction and giving patterns. You may find information in the library stacks or you may wish to complete electronic searches through a variety of databases. Today, many campuses have electronic access to library resources across the country and around the world. Use this information to become informed, which will ultimately enable you to develop a better survey instrument.

One word of caution with respect to locally prepared survey questionnaires concerns the issue of validity and reliability. Experience shows that audiences sometimes view the credibility of survey results on a proportional scale with the extent to which they are hearing what they want to hear. If the data show something other than the anticipated result, studies have been criticized on technical issues such as instrument reliability, validity, sampling error, and nonresponse bias.

Depending on the survey content, the survey results, and the technical sophistication of the audience, institutional researchers may find it necessary to calculate reliability coefficients, as well as some estimates of sampling and

31

nonsampling error. Good discussions of these and other survey research topics are available in the Suskie monograph and the other books cited as resources in this section.

Profitable references about the survey research include:

Kalton, G. (1984). *Introduction to Survey Sampling*. Beverly Hills: Sage Publications.

Babbie, E. R. (1973). *Survey Research Methods*. Belmont, CA: Wadsworth Publishing Company, Inc.

Bradburn, N. M., & Sudman S. (1988). *Polls and Surveys: Understanding What They Tell Us*. San Francisco: Jossey-Bass, Inc.

Suskie, L. A. (1992). *Questionnaire Survey Research: What Works*. Tallahassee, FL: Association for Institutional Research.

D. Internal Data Sources

While the majority of this section has concerned data from external sources that are available to the researcher, it is wise not to overlook additional information that is available within the institution. Valuable sources of data for individual college studies are: the President's Annual Report, the annual report of senior cabinet members, and departmental annual reports; the institution's annual financial statement, as well as the periodic audit from an external accounting firm. Equally valuable for historical or current information are institutional and program self-study documents and planning documents prepared by individual departments.

Institutional research offices are usually involved in data analysis or the data generation for many of these documents, but may not receive the final product. It can often be useful to obtain copies, not only for data verification purposes, but for subsequent use as data sources.

Some of the most significant resources needed to perform effective institutional research have been presented in this chapter: books, journals, and monographs; professional associations; computer resources; external data sources, commercially and locally prepared surveys, and some internal data sources. The next chapters discuss several concrete strategies and approaches to utilize these resources in a comprehensive institutional research program.

CHAPTER THREE:
KEY RESPONSIBILITIES OF AN INSTITUTIONAL
RESEARCHER

Although no two institutional researchers proceed through the work day completing the same exact tasks, there are several job responsibilities that are quite similar within the diverse array of institutional operations across higher education. Frequently, the size of a school's institutional research staff will determine the breadth and variety of issues that will be examined. Nevertheless, virtually all institutional researchers are involved with or have responsibilities in the following areas: general data collection and reporting (e.g., student and employee counts, graduation rates, demographic trends, etc.), retention and enrollment management, interinstitutional peer analyses, assessment, and budget support. This chapter discusses general data collection, enrollment management, and peer analysis. Due to the variety of information related to assessment and budget support, these areas are discussed in Chapters 4 through 6.

I. General Data Collection and Reporting

Many institutional research offices serve as a storehouse for the numbers available to describe an institution. Typically, institutional researchers collect baseline data on students, faculty and staff, facilities, finances, and other information on the external environment.[1] Basic descriptive statistics such as the number of male and female students and employees, students' ethnic distribution, financial aid recipients, in-state versus out-of-state students, number of degrees awarded, student credit hours, and grade point distribution reports are some of the data that are routinely collected.

The institutional research office, therefore, is the logical choice to report and distribute institutional information to external agencies such as the federal government (e.g., IPEDS), regional accrediting associations, other higher education institutions, and companies which are assembling information for publication (e.g., College Board, Barron's, Peterson's Guide and other surveys).

---

[1] Note that many of the possible measures of these items are included in Chapter 1, Table 1.

Often, institutional researchers are responsible for the annual preparation of a Factbook which supplies key information about their institution. Since the Factbook is usually an annual event, as is reporting to the various external agencies, it is important that these data be collected in a systematic and timely manner to ensure consistency from term to term. A good way to collect this data is through standard production reports.

A. Standard Production Reports

A production report simply refers to computer code that generates information from an institution's database. The information that is needed may exist, for example, in the schools' student records system, personnel file, admissions file, financial aid database, or even a combination of files. The program simply reads the required information in the appropriate file and generates a report or table that gives the desired data. The work for the institutional researcher is limited to a request to "run" the necessary program(s).

Depending on the institutional researcher's programming ability, it may be necessary to request assistance from the campus computing center's programming staff. Computing centers generally have technical staff who can program a report to the specifications set out by the institutional researchers. Appendix 2 shows sample pages from two standard production reports at the University of Delaware.

Many institutional research offices report enrollment and other counts at the beginning of a fall (and perhaps, spring) term. Typically, institutional managers agree on what the official report date shall be. At this point, student and employee data is "frozen," or designated as the official file from which production reports are run. This frozen data file provides the data for all "official" internal and external enrollment reports such as those required by federal and state agencies. Note that the extract data file is retained on line and may subsequently be used to run a report from the official numbers at any time.

It is, of course, possible for student enrollment and other information to change after the official date. This points out the sometimes disconcerting difference between an official report date and current levels. It is important to distinguish between these two concepts because, depending on the question which is asked, the institutional researcher may need the frozen data file or the current (and technically more accurate) data.

If standard reports are not already in production, keep in mind the added benefit of sharing reports with others on campus. If the production reports are cumbersome and not easy to read, it may be necessary to complete an intermediate step of compiling a second, less complex table of data for colleagues. If the production reports are easy to read, they can be copied as they appear and sent directly to other units at the institution.

A second way to distribute enrollment management information successfully across campus is to create a student profile report. This type of report can be easily generated from the official data set that is extracted from the Student Records System at the beginning of each major term. A student profile report can be generated using the SPSS Tables or SAS Tabulate procedure. (SPSS TABLES is an additional module available at extra cost from the basic SPSS package.)

With this powerful statistical software, an "official" profile of all students can be generated for any given term. The profile gives users a quick summary of the key information typically needed at the beginning of the term: How many students are enrolled? What is the class breakdown of undergraduates? How many minority students are enrolled this term? What departments or majors enrolled the greatest number of freshmen? These and other questions are answered on the Student Profile in a format which is easy for other administrators to digest.

B. Ad Hoc Requests

Because institutional research often becomes the central location for information about the institution, the office may receive a multitude of ad hoc questions, surveys, and requests. The variety of questions that are received is tremendously diverse. Questions can range from the number of faculty/staff employed three or four decades ago, or the number of employees who were born in one county of the state, to questions about the number of philosophy courses taken by a entire graduating cohort at any time over their undergraduate career.

Although many ad hoc questions are unique questions that may never again be asked, it is useful to compile a file of these requests. If a similar question is posed by someone else at the institution, a whole new response may not have to be created. Or at least, the researcher may have a good starting point for how to answer the new question. The important point to remember is that institutional researchers should have at their disposal the means to answer ad hoc questions quickly, whatever this requires given the internal dynamics of the institution.

II. Enrollment Management

Enrollment management in the area of higher education broadly refers to topics that are related to student enrollments. Key issues, for example, include admissions recruitment, marketing, tuition pricing, financial aid, and retention and attrition research. Some writers also include topics such as student opinion, satisfaction, and program evaluation in the area of enrollment management.

The ratios of in-state to out-of state students and its attendant affect on tuition revenue, or the successful retention of students is paramount to many administrators within an institution. Most institutional researchers supply data for and/or are involved in decisions which guide admissions goals and decisions and therefore are involved in enrollment management. This section highlights some of the major components of enrollment management and relates these components to the I-P-O framework presented in Chapter 1.

A. Inputs

Recruitment. There are three central components to any admissions cycle: the number of applications, the number of offers of admission, and the number of deposits. These components lend themselves to the development of two key ratios: offers of admission as a percentage of total applications (commonly referred to as "offer rate"), and paid deposits as a percentage of total offers (commonly referred to as the "yield rate"). Offer and yield rates are crucial to enrollment planning.

A weekly admissions report (see Appendix 3) can be used to show the number of applicants, acceptances, denials, and enrolling students. As well, the report can be programmed to generate SAT averages and other statistics.[2] Appendix 3 is another example of a standardized production report. The report compares application statistics for approximately the same date for three separate years. This type of weekly report is helpful because it allows the institution to manage enrollment decisions. If yield rates are relatively stable,

---

[2]The PGI statistics found in Appendix 3 stands for predicted grade index. It is a computation of an individual applicant's predicted freshman grades based on their high school grade point average and SAT scores. The weights applied to this high school information is obtained through a traditional SAT predictive viability study which can be conducted by an individual institution or with the assistance of the Validity Study Service, a unit of the Educational Testing Service.

it is possible to determine the number of admission offers that must be made to bring in the desired class size. Similarly, trend data in offer rates suggest the number of applications that must be achieved to obtain an offer pool of sufficient size to yield the desired paid deposits.

For example, if the target freshman class size is 1,000 and yield rates historically have approximated 43%, then a minimum of 2,325 offers would have to be made (divide 1,000 by 0.43 to arrive at 2,325). Similarly, if offer rates have historically clustered around 50%, then a minimum of 4,650 applications would have to be received to produce the offer pool of 2,325. Admissions personnel and institutional researchers use these data as benchmarks for annual recruitment planning.

The second page of Appendix 3 shows in detail how enrollment targets are being achieved. The page lists information on the number of students set as the enrollment target, the previous year's yield, the number of applicants who must be admitted based on the previous yield, and the current number of students who have been offered admissions. This information is extremely valuable in enabling the admission office to meet enrollment targets. If the yield falls off drastically in a given year, for example, mid-course corrections can be made by admitting additional applicants. Note also that this report can be calculated down to the major level if this type of detail is needed.

A weekly admissions summary usually focuses on basic counts and overall averages, which does not allow for an accurate picture of trends in the "quality" of applicants. Appendix 4 shows a three year trend analysis of admissions activity, in which applicants are sorted by SAT Verbal, Math, and Combined scores. In this Admissions Monitoring Report, it is evident that yield rates vary significantly across intervals of student quality. Any attempt to increase the number of more academically prepared students will require adjustments in the number of applications and offers. Solid trend data can provide guideposts for establishing application and offer targets.

This kind of Admissions Monitoring Report can be produced weekly from September through June, and allows a comparison of offer and yield rates at comparable points in time within the cycle over a period of years; the table can be produced for any week in the cycle. The report is generated directly off the mainframe by means of fourth generation language code (in this case, NATURAL), but could also be produced on an electronic spreadsheet by downloading appropriate data elements from the Admissions Database on the mainframe computer.

The capability to predict accurately the size of incoming freshman classes is essential to effective management of student body enrollments. That accurate prediction can be achieved with effective monitoring of admissions activity.

Financial Aid. The effective utilization of financial aid resources is also an important component of enrollment management. This has become even more important in the recent past as tuition and fees charges have increased, institutional financial aid budgets have soared, and federal and state funding sources have declined.

Relatively few studies have analyzed the relationships between financial aid awards, student academic quality, and applicants' enrollment decisions. Some excellent reading about financial aid and its impact on students' enrollment and persistence decisions are:

Scannell, J. (1992). *The Effect of Financial Aid Policies on Admission and Enrollment*. New York: College Entrance Examination Board.

Scannell presents a useful and practical analysis of how higher education institutions can think about admissions and the financial aid process. Other helpful analyses are:

Cabrera, A. & Castaneda, M. (1992). The role of finances in the persistence process: A structural model. *Research in Higher Education, 33* (5), 571-594.

Wilcox. L. (1991). Evaluating the impact of financial aid on student recruitment and retention. In D. Hossler (Ed.), *Evaluating Student Recruitment and Retention Programs, New Directions for Institutional Research, No. 70*, Jossey-Bass, Inc.

Chapman, R., & Jackson, R. (1987). *College Choices of Academically Able Students: The Influence of No-Need Financial Aid and Other Factors*. New York: College Entrance Examination Board.

St. John, E. (1985). The influence of student aid on persistence. *Journal of Student Financial Aid, 19*, 52-68.

Institutional researchers are now being called on to study important financial aid questions such as: 1) How do financial aid awards relate to students' enrollment decisions? Is the institution receiving the greatest benefits from the expenditure of financial aid funds? 2) What relationship do scholarships and financial aid have on the quality of the freshman class? 3) In which programs or majors is financial aid distributed? 4) Would different ratios of loan and self-help improve recruitment. How much tuition discounting is necessary?

B. Process

Retention Rates. Most colleges and universities target as a primary goal, students' successful graduation. For two-year schools, some students enroll who do not intend to graduate. Consequently, these institutions may want to separate degree-seeking and non degree-seeking students, or to track successful transfer rates to four-year institutions.

Because persistence is so closely tied to the institutional mission, especially at four-year institutions, many college administrators are critically concerned about student persistence rates. Perhaps the most fundamental measure of student process is whether students graduate. Institutional research offices have traditionally used cohort survival analyses to monitor student retention, attrition, and graduation patterns.

Appendix 5 depicts a typical cohort survival analysis for 10 different freshman cohorts at one institution. The table displays dropout and retention rates for each year following admission, as well as graduation rates. For example, of the 2,988 freshmen admitted in Fall 1983, 83.6% persisted into the sophomore year; 16.4% were lost to attrition during the same time. The data show that by the time that the Fall 1988 freshman cohort entered the institution, the attrition rate had dropped to 13.7%. The graduation rate for the Fall 1983 cohort finished at 69.4%; subsequent cohorts graduate about seven out of ten individuals who entered as freshmen.

These data are essential for two reasons. First, they reveal the extent to which the institution fulfills its mission of graduating entering freshmen. Second, the data are critical to solid enrollment planning. Stable attrition and retention rates enable enrollment planners to arrive at reasonable estimates of the number of entering freshmen who will remain at the institution until graduation, and the length of time that it will take to get there.

By reading the columns in Appendix 5 from top to bottom, trend data for attrition and retention are available for each of the four to six years that an entering freshman cohort remains at a college or university. By examining these data the researcher can compute attrition, retention, and transition (movement from one fall to the next) coefficients for a basic student flow model. Student flow is the key to effective enrollment management. It answers three questions:

1. Of those students who entered the institution, how many will remain until graduation?

2. How many will leave the institution without graduating? For two-year schools emphasizing transfer, how many successfully transfer to another institution?

3. For those persisting, how long will it take to graduate?

Reliable answers to these questions, based on cohort survival analysis, enable more accurate estimation of student body size at any given point in time. These estimates, in turn, are essential for accurate revenue forecasting and staffing projections. Cohort survival is a basic tool in institutional research, and one which the practitioner should know.

A retention analysis can be produced annually by running a report which traces term by term enrollment for each member of an entering freshman cohort (e.g., all first-time freshmen who enrolled in Fall, 1985). The report examines whether the student is matriculated and/or graduated in any subsequent term from the initial point of entry. These data can be entered into an electronic spreadsheet which automatically updates the table.

Additional tables can be produced separately for gender, ethnicity, in-state/non-resident status, transfer students, and first-time freshmen. These more detailed reports can enable you to explore specific subsets within the student body where attrition rates may be excessively high, and which would otherwise be hidden in a general analysis of all students. This, in turn, can improve enrollment planning capabilities.

III. Peer Institutions

Institutional researchers frequently have the responsibility to develop a group of peer institutions and collect information about this group. Data on comparative institutional pricing, financial aid, faculty compensation, revenues and expenditures, and other facts are often useful to institutional managers for planning and decision-making. For example, in considering tuition increases, it is helpful to have historical benchmarks of tuition increases at competitor institutions. Similarly, a comparison of percentage increases in revenue and expenditure streams can provide information on areas in which the institution may be doing well or not as well as others. Comparative data on faculty and staff salaries is also very important for the institution.

Teeter and Brinkman (1992) note that the literature on peer institutions can be divided into two broad categories: the methodology for selection of peer institutions and the usefulness of comparison groups. Although a variety of analytical techniques are available for peer group selection, oftentimes the selection of peer institutions are made on common sense kinds of grounds: student body size, total educational and general expenditures or Carnegie classification. Other times, the selection criteria may serve political purposes. As well, organizations such as NCHEMS can assist (for a fee) institutions in the development of a group of peer institutions.

Since a fairly well-established literature exists on the selection and use of peer institutions, and since space is limited here, readers are referred to the excellent source cited in the shaded box. Also note that Chapter 2 previously discussed several national data exchanges which can provide a source for timely, comparative information. In addition, Chapters 5 and 6 contain brief examples of using financial information of peer institutions to inform campus planning and decision-making.

For information on peer institutions, readers are referred to the following excellent article and the sources listed in it:

Teeter, D., & Brinkman, P. (1992). Peer institutions. In Whitely, M., Porter, J., & Fenske, R. (Eds.). *The Primer for Institutional Research.* Tallahassee: Florida: The Association for Institutional Research.

Summary

This chapter has presented some of the basic tasks that comprise the work of many institutional research offices. Central among these are data collection, storage, and reporting (both internal, external, and "ad hoc"), enrollment management issues such as marketing and student retention, and the concept of peer institutions. Although institutional researchers and their home institutions may place greatly different weights on these subjects, they should be a part of every researcher's vocabulary.

CHAPTER FOUR:
ASSESSMENT IN INSTITUTIONAL RESEARCH

Introduction to the Concept of Assessment in Institutional Research

Although assessment has been part of higher education for centuries, it is only within the past decade or two that assessment has become a demanding topic that touches every institutional researcher. The current level of interest about assessment is propelled by concerned parents, lawmakers, and students. All but fourteen state legislatures have or are considering the implementation of campus assessment programs (National Governor's Association, 1988, in Davis, 1989). In 1991, the American Council on Education found 81% of all colleges surveyed had assessment activities in place, up from 55% in 1988. And Muffo (1992) reported that 80% of all NASULGC institutions were engaged in assessment efforts.

Think about these possible scenarios:

• Your institution is preparing for its next accreditation visit and you have been asked to prepare a summary of student attitudes and level of satisfaction with campus programs and services;

• A faculty member asks for your help in measuring student cognitive gains;

• A colleague in Housing & Residence Life asks for help in assessing moral and ethical development of residence hall students;

• Your provost wants evaluative data on the effectiveness of a new freshman year experience program that is scheduled to be implemented next year.

• Members of the Board of Trustees/Regents are concerned about the drop in number of new student applications. Members of the Board believe that your institution should lower standards to enable more students to be admitted. You are asked to help analyze the situation and offer a suggestion.

The primary goal of any assessment program is the evaluation and improvement of some aspect of higher education. Assessment may concern the performance of individuals, student or employee groups, the effectiveness of instructional practices, or the functioning of departments. Student assessment encompasses a wide variety of activities such as determining cognitive gains through pre- and post measures, evaluating programs and curricula, mastery of content, student satisfaction, and development of personal and social skills.

Some campus officials view assessment more narrowly, emphasizing student learning, skill enhancement, and outcomes. Boyer and Ewell (1988) define assessment as "processes that provide information about individual students, curricula, or programs, institutions, or about entire systems of institutions." In myriad forms, it may be formative (aimed at improvement of what is already being done) or summative (for making decisions about resources, institutions, or persons within an institution), and can focus on students, staff, programs, or institutions. As an institutional researcher you are likely to be involved in assessment efforts at your institution. The methodology and choice of measurements will depend upon the group in focus.

When initiating an assessment project, the following questions may be pertinent: What are the purposes of this assessment? How does this project fit with other assessment projects that have been completed recently? (e.g., is there an overall plan for how we are assessing our students, staff, and programs?) Should qualitative or quantitative measures (or both) be incorporated? Must this project be submitted to the human subjects board for approval? To whom will the results be reported? How will the results be used? What will happen if the results are bad news for the institution?

Three important references for research on college student development are:

Astin. A. (1993). *What Matters in College.* San Francisco: Jossey-Bass.

Pascarella, E. & Terenzini, P. (1990). *How College Affects Students.* San Francisco: Jossey-Bass, Inc.

Tinto, V. (1987). *Leaving College: Rethinking the Causes and Cures of Student Attrition.* Chicago: University of Chicago Press.

Once these questions have been answered, your chances of success will be greatly increased. It is vital that you understand why this assessment is taking place (i.e., is it a state or institutional mandate; sincere interest in better understanding student growth and development; an agenda for curricular reform?). The decision to use qualitative or quantitative measures (or both) will depend on your goals for this assessment as well as your resources. Quantitative methods, most often in the form of one or more surveys, can yield large amounts of data with minimal effort. Qualitative methods, including case studies, interviews, participant observation, and portfolio assessment can offer tremendously rich data but usually require extensive time commitments. Some researchers have found that the combination of qualitative and quantitative methods often provide the most comprehensive picture of the quality of life on a campus.

A key element of any assessment program is high quality (and therefore useful) information. A smaller, well-planned and tightly controlled study may yield more usable data than a larger, half-thought-out study that has little sense of direction. Any assessment effort must begin with clarification of reasons why the study is being conducted, identifying the information that is needed, determining the procedures, implementing plans, and ending with utilizing the information gained as the basis for implementing plans for change.

Many references on assessment in higher education are available for your review including:

Banta, T.W. (Ed.) (1988). *Implementing Outcomes Assessment: Promise and Perils. New Directions for Institutional Research, No. 59.* San Francisco: Jossey-Bass, Inc.

Boyer, E. & Ewell, P.T. (1988). *State-based Approaches to Assessment in Undergraduate Education: A Glossary and Selected References.* Denver, CO: Education Commission of the United States.

Bray, D. & Belcher, M.J. (Eds.). (1987). *Issues in Student Assessment. New Directions for Community Colleges, No. 59.* San Francisco: Jossey-Bass, Inc.

Davis, B.G. (1989). Demystifying assessment: Learning from the field of evaluation. In P. J. Gray (Ed.). *Achieving Assessment Goals Using Evaluation Techniques, New Directions for Higher Education, No. 67.* San Francisco: Jossey-Bass, Inc.

Ewell, P.T. (Ed.) (1985). *Assessing Educational Outcomes. New Directions for Institutional Research, No. 47.* San Francisco: Jossey-Bass, Inc.

Fendley, W.R. & Seeloff, L.T. (1993). *Reference Sources: An Annotated Bibliography.* Tallahassee: Association for Institutional Research.

Fetterman, D.M. (1991). *Using Qualitative Methods in Institutional Research. New Directions for Institutional Research, No. 72.* San Francisco: Jossey-Bass, Inc.

Gray, P.T. (Ed.) (1989). *Achieving Assessment Goals Using Evaluation Techniques. New Directions for Higher Education, No. 67.* San Francisco: Jossey-Bass, Inc.

Halpern, D.F. (Ed.) (1987). *Student Outcomes Assessment: What Institutions Stand to Gain. New Directions for Higher Education, No. 59.* San Francisco: Jossey-Bass, Inc.

Heywood, J. (1989). *Assessment in Higher Education.* New York: John Wiley & Sons.

Muffo, J.A. (1992). The status of student outcomes assessment in NASULGC member institutions. *Research in Higher Education, 33, (6),* 765-774.

Noel, L., Levitz, R., & Saluri, D. (Eds.) (1985). *Increasing Student Retention.* San Francisco: Jossey-Bass, Inc.

Terenzini, P. (1984). Assessment with open eyes: Pitfalls in studying student outcomes. *Journal of Higher Education,* 60 (6), 644-664.

Davis (1989) reports six general steps to take in any assessment:

1) focus the evaluation by identifying goals and restraints from the client;
2) identify stakeholders and audiences;
3) generate questions of interest to the stakeholders;
4) refine and limit questions through negotiation with the vested parties;
5) determine the methodology: for each question specify the instrument or data source, the sample from whom data have been or need to be collected, the time frame for collection of data, methods of analysis, and the intended use of the results; and
6) communicate the findings to stakeholders in ways that they can use the results.

Clearly, a thoughtful and planned approach is necessary for anyone who considers undertaking any assessment project. The reader is reminded that inputs, process, and outputs, as components of an open system, are not assessed and measured in isolation; it is their relationship with the organizational environment that is crucial.

From an institutional perspective, assessment can be either cross-sectional or longitudinal in nature and can fall into two broad categories: 1) student outcomes and 2) institutional or personnel assessment. Within these two broad categories there are many assessment projects that can be described within the input-process-output model (I-P-O) discussed in Chapter One. In some instances, one assessment issue may be intended as a process measure, while in another instance it may be intended as an output measure. Figure 2 shows the relationship of assessment projects or issues in the I-P-O model.

I. Student Assessment

Figure 2 shows that student assessment occurs at many points throughout the students' involvement with a college or university. Prior to or very early in the students' first term, many college officials wish to obtain academic, demographic, or attitudinal information on students. This can easily be accomplished through the administration of one or more surveys to all or a random sample of students. Three common ways of obtaining this information are discussed below:

Figure 2: Possible Interactions of Measures in I-P-O Model

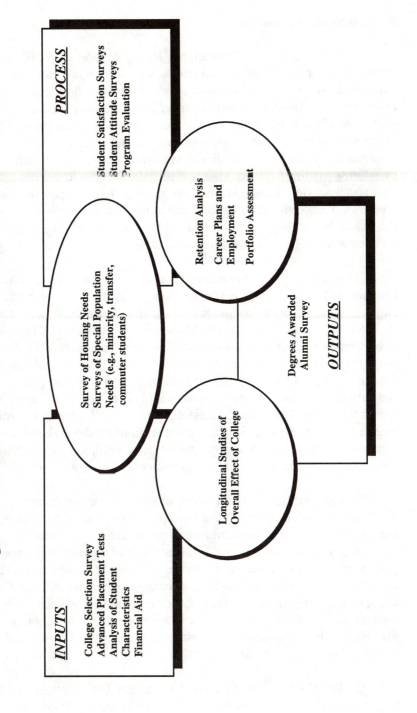

INPUTS

College Selection Survey
Advanced Placement Tests
Analysis of Student
Characteristics
Financial Aid

Survey of Housing Needs
Surveys of Special Population
Needs (e.g., minority, transfer,
commuter students)

Longitudinal Studies of
Overall Effect of College

PROCESS

Student Satisfaction Surveys
Student Attitude Surveys
Program Evaluation

Retention Analysis
Career Plans and
Employment
Portfolio Assessment

Degrees Awarded
Alumni Survey

OUTPUTS

A. New Student Assessment

1. The Cooperative Institutional Research Program (CIRP) <u>Student Information Form (SIF)</u> provides a profile of an institution's entering freshman class with respect to educational plans and attitudinal and behavioral characteristics. An added benefit is that an institution can compare its freshman student profile with nationally-normed samples of college freshmen. The SIF questionnaire also collects basic demographic and attitudinal data, as well as information on students' educational and career plans. It is a useful tool for monitoring entering freshmen classes at periodic intervals to determine whether demographics (i.e., family income, religious preference, parental education levels, etc.), educational aspirations, and attitudes have changed. This allows the researcher to suggest possible modifications to existing programs and services which relate to current freshman classes.

The SIF allows researchers to assess the extent to which a given institution's freshman class is similar to the freshman classes throughout the nation in general, and at institutions similar in size and mission to one's own. In 1968, Alexander Astin, of the University of California at Los Angeles, developed the Cooperative Institutional Research Program (CIRP). The CIRP is a nationally representative group of colleges and universities who administer the Student Information Form to new students, generally first-time freshmen, and submit the completed forms to Astin and his associates for analysis. The research staff at CIRP annually produces a national "Profile of the American Freshman," and provide to participating institutions the national norms for responses to the survey items, by total (all freshmen), and by institution type (i.e., university or four year college, public or private, and so on).

The Student Information Form is moderately expensive (approximately $2.00 per student) to purchase and have processed. Experience suggests that annual administration of the instrument is not necessary; the results do not shift dramatically from year to year. Administration of the survey at three to four year intervals may be a more viable strategy. The instrument may also be used in following student cohorts to assess changes in attitudes and beliefs which might be indirectly ascribed to the college experience. Specimen copies of the Student Information Form, and other CIRP materials, may be obtained from: The Higher Education Research Institute, University of California at Los Angeles, Los Angeles, California 90024.

2. The College Board's <u>Admitted Student Questionnaire</u> (ASQ). A fundamental component of admissions enrollment research is the assessment of applicants' attitudes about the college and universities to which they apply.

Developed with the assistance of national admissions and marketing experts, The College Board offers a comprehensive admissions marketing survey. In general, the ASQ seeks to answer some basic questions:

- What characteristics of the institution and its competitors impact students' enrollment decisions?

- Why do some students choose to attend this institution over other colleges and universities? Compared to the competition, what is the institution doing well, and what, if anything, is it doing badly?

- Who is the competition?

- What is the college's overall "image?"

- What are the most important sources of information applicants draw on to support their college decision?

- Are there significant "attitudinal" differences between enrolling and non-enrolling students?

- How do financial aid offers impact applicants' enrollment decisions?

The ASQ is made up of seven sections. The first part of the questionnaire lists 20 characteristics of colleges and universities (e.g., quality of faculty, variety of courses, athletic programs, access to off-campus cultural opportunities), and asks the applicant to indicate how important these attributes are and how the college compared to others that were considered.

The next two sections of the ASQ generate information about whose opinions influenced the student's college selection decision and which information sources were utilized by the student (e.g., visit to campus, contact with coaches or current students). In both of these sections, the students indicate how important the specific source was and how the school compared to others institutions that were considered.

The fourth section of the survey lets the student communicate their impression of the overall institutional "image." The ASQ provides 24 words or phrases (e.g., personal, intense, isolated, back-up school, average, exciting) that when combined, generate a specific college or university image. The fifth part of the questionnaire provides information about the admissions competition, who the competitors are, whether the student was admitted and/or offered

51

financial aid. The sixth part of the ASQ provides further detail on cost and financial aid issues: comparison of total "out-of-pocket" cost with other schools that were considered and the portion of the financial aid package that was scholarship or grant.

The final section of the survey provides general background information (e.g., gender, ethnicity, high school grade point average) which allows the researcher to conduct more specific research analyses. (For example, do private school students perceive the institution differently than public school students? Do women have the same attitudes about the institution as males?) Student gender, ethnicity, permanent residence, academic preparedness as measured by self-reported high school grade point average and SAT scores, are all useful subgroups for analysis.

The Admitted Student Questionnaire is an excellent tool for understanding and coping with the admissions marketplace in a competitive era. Other advantages to utilizing the College Board survey is that results are provided in the form of two reports. The "Highlights Report" summarizes main findings, and the "Detailed Report" gives the frequency distribution of all items on the survey. Thus, the institutional researcher does not have to spend time having the survey items transferred to computer, verify data entry, write software code that analyzes the survey, and summarize the results.

Hundreds of colleges and universities have now used the ASQ and normative data are available. The College Board provides a norms report as part of the basic service, but it also possible to request normative data on specific subsets of institutional competitors. Institutional researchers may also purchase the survey data on tape or disk for further analyses.

3. Conducting this type of marketing analysis over time may enable the Admissions Office to customize recruiting strategies for different market components and to better position the institution within the overall marketplace. If financing a published survey such as the ASQ is a concern, it is also possible to administer a locally-developed survey. The College Selection Survey (CSS) developed at the University of Delaware is one such example. A copy of the College Selection Survey is found in Appendix 6. The College Selection Survey can easily be administered to a randomly selected sample of students who have been offered admission to the institution. Although the out-of-pocket costs for a locally developed survey may be somewhat less than the cost to purchase a commercial product, researchers also need to consider the staff time that must be spent on coding, data analysis, and report preparation.

B. Enrolled Student Assessment

The extent to which students use and are pleased with the programs and services offered by a college or university is a major force in shaping their decision to remain at the institution, or to leave and pursue their studies elsewhere. Data collection instruments which measure student opinion can be obtained from the Educational Testing Service and the American College Testing Program or other test publishers. Listed below are a few good examples:

1. Student Opinion Survey This relatively short instrument, developed by the American College Testing Program (ACT), is used frequently by institutional researchers and is easy for students to complete. It is divided into four sections. Section One asks for basic demographic data from the respondent.

Section Two arrays 23 programs and services typically found at a college or university, ranging from academic advising, library, computing, and other academically oriented services to health service, parking, and day care. Respondents are asked if they used the service, and if so, how satisfied they were. The question about actual use is critical for accurate analysis; it enables the researcher to discard responses from those who did not personally use a service but nonetheless assign it a satisfaction rating based on hearsay.

Section Three lists 42 separate characteristics of the college environment and asks for satisfaction ratings. The characteristics fall within six major groupings: academic (e.g. availability of faculty, faculty attitudes toward students, quality of academic advising); admissions (e.g., general admissions procedures, availability of financial aid); rules and regulations (e.g., student voice in college policies, discipline code); facilities (e.g. quality of classrooms, laboratories, study areas); registration (general registration procedures, billing and fee payment policies); and a general category (e.g., concern for students as individuals, attitude of non-teaching staff toward students).

Section Four is composed of 30 items locally prepared by the home institution. Issues not addressed by American College Testing on the pre-printed form can be included in Section Four. Finally, there is space in Section Four for the respondent to add written comments on the general topic of student satisfaction. A specimen set of Student Opinion Survey materials can be purchased from American College Testing at the address provided in Chapter Two.

Many institutions opt to use the survey processing services offered by American College Testing. For a fee, the institution receives a printed computerized analysis of the survey responses, national norms for those responses arrayed by institutional type, a computer tape of the University's data, and a file layout of the tape for further analysis with a statistical software package. Other vendors provide similar services for their questionnaires.

Once the instruments have been scored, mean scores for institutional data can be compared with national norms, testing for statistically significant differences on responses to each item. Data comparisons with national norms allow the researcher to ascertain whether response patterns for a specific item from their students are typical of all students in similar institutions or differ from the norms group. Comparing responses between students who persist and students who leave can help in focusing on areas of strong dissatisfaction or possible areas for skill building among those students who leave.

Utilization of an instrument such as the Student Opinion Survey also permits a novel way for an institutional researcher to conduct an attrition analysis. Typically the survey is administered in the spring semester. The institutional research office can wait until the following fall and, using the student identification numbers provided by respondents on the spring survey, separate the respondent pool into two groups – respondents who completed the survey in the Spring and did register in the Fall, and respondents who completed the survey but did not register and did not graduate. The responses from persisters and dropouts may then be compared for statistically significant differences.

2. College Student Experiences Questionnaire (CSEQ)   While student satisfaction analyses describe student satisfaction levels with programs and services they have used, the College Student Experiences Questionnaire gets at a different aspect of student "process" – how students use their time during college, and whether the college experience has changed them. Developed at The University of California at Los Angeles and administered at institutions throughout the country, the CSEQ is an excellent complement to surveys that focus on student satisfaction. Different versions for two- and four-year institutions are available. A sample copy of the College Student Experiences Questionnaire may be obtained from: Center for the Study of Evaluation, Graduate School of Education, University of California at Los Angeles, Los Angeles, California 90024.

The CSEQ collects several different types of information. Demographic or "independent" variables go well beyond the traditional age, sex, or ethnicity choices (although they are collected as well). Demographic data include parents' educational levels, amount of time actually spent each week in school-related activity, amount of parental financial support, amount of time spent working at a job while in school, and so on. These provide a solid background profile of the respondent pool.

The questionnaire then asks students to report their level of involvement in various library experiences, in contact with faculty in varied settings, in various learning activities within courses, in arts activities, and in student and athletic activities. Experience in writing, mathematics, science, and technological activities, and in personal and general student acquaintances are also explored. These data, combined with information on what students read about and talk about, provide a richly textured context for studying the "value added" dimension of student process. Respondents characterize the intellectual dimensions of their college experience and estimate gains along several curricular and extracurricular dimensions.

Like the Student Opinion Survey, the CSEQ comes with national normative data by institutional type. And like the student satisfaction analysis described above, the CSEQ can be analyzed for statistically significant differences between institutional and national response patterns and, within the single institution, for differences between persisters and dropouts. The comprehensive body of data from students who are satisfied or dissatisfied with the programs and services of an institution, combined with data on how students spend their time and how those activities affect them, presents an excellent picture of how students are changed by the total college experience.

The CSEQ offers a wealth of information about students. Results at The University of Delaware, for example, found that, in general, self-reported gains in academic and personal skills paralleled those of students from the doctoral norms group and were generally greater for females and for students with higher grades (Bauer, 1992). In addition, results have shown that native students report greater gains and invest more effort into their college experiences than transfer students. Freshmen report the highest levels of overall satisfaction, and seniors report making the greatest gains in academic and personal skills development.

Use of the CSEQ or other similar instruments may lead the institutional researcher to other studies. Beginning in fall 1993, for example, the Office of Institutional Research at the University of Delaware began collecting data for a longitudinal study of college students. The major purpose for this study is to learn more about how and when students change as they move through their undergraduate experience. Institutional researchers at this institution hope to better define levels of academic and social ability as students begin their freshman year, to identify what activities are consuming time and energy, how students perceive the college environment, how much students are satisfied with that environment, and most importantly, how they are changing over time.

If one chooses to not use one of the available published instruments, a locally-designed instrument may meet an institution's unique needs. The primary advantages of locally-designed and produced instruments are the ability to use questions that most specifically relate to your own campus and the potential for some cost savings. The primary disadvantage is the lack of established norms and reliability estimates that may have to determined locally. Listed below are some examples of locally prepared instruments that have been developed at one or more institutions.

3. SUNY-Albany Surveys - The Office of Institutional Research at the State University of New York (SUNY) at Albany has developed several satisfaction/needs assessment instruments as well as an alumni survey that have been used with SUNY-Albany students since 1978. The Freshman Survey administered to students in early fall obtains general demographic information as well as attitudinal data. Data are collected on what opportunities students think they will be involved in during their college experience, and what areas of help students believe they need.

The Student Experiences questionnaires (Freshman and Senior Year Follow-Up) identify what activities students have engaged in, satisfaction with the institution, and self-reported estimates for growth in a variety of academic and social skills. The Alumni Survey obtains general information on such areas as educational degrees completed, a brief job history, current annual income, and overall satisfaction with their college experience since graduation. In addition, the Alumni Survey asks respondents to indicate the current level of importance of a variety of cognitive and social skills needed for current endeavors and how much these skills were enhanced as a result of their attendance at the institution. For more information, contact Dr. J. Fredericks Volkwein, Director of Institutional Research, State University of New York at Albany, Albany, NY 12222.

4. Student Needs Survey - As part of an institutional researcher's likely involvement with campus colleagues, it is possible to become involved in the development and/or analysis of student academic, personal, or social skills. As an example, a survey of student needs was developed at the University of Pittsburgh in cooperation with Psychological Assessment Resources, Inc., and modified at the University of Delaware. The instrument was designed to

determine the level of student need for various career, personal, and learning skills. This instrument offers an extensive amount of information on non-intellectual student needs and can be especially helpful to staff members involved with student needs outside the classroom.

5. Exit Survey or Interview - Many officials would like to know why students in good standing leave their institution prior to degree completion. An exit interview or survey is one opportunity to acquire some of this information. Because many students do not announce their departure (often we find out only after the student fails to register for the following term), a one-to-one interview or survey may yield information for a relatively small portion of the exiting students. While some schools mail a survey to non-returning students, others attempt to talk to students before they leave. A project at the University of Tennessee, for example, required students to participate in an exit interview with a trained upperclass student before a tuition refund, release of transcript, or Dean's signature for release was granted.

6. Portfolio Assessment - The use of portfolios, especially for some disciplines, has been standard practice for some time, but the notion of the portfolio as a broader qualitative measure, is now gaining momentum to help students in many fields document their cognitive gains over time from matriculation to graduation. Used as an employment tool, a portfolio may contain a student's best work, but as a broader assessment tool, the academic portfolio is linked to program goals of the department or college and documents a students' level of writing and cognitive skills at entry and at graduation.

The initial design and implementation of this type of assessment can be lengthy, and faculty must be committed to developing guidelines and evaluative criteria as well as providing student support. The benefits, however, greatly outweigh the time and effort involved. The process facilitates synthesis of one's work near graduation, students are more likely to be more careful in developing their undergraduate curriculum, and when material is prepared for the portfolio from outside the classroom, there is an integration of learning experiences that are course-related and extracurricular (Bunda, in Fetterman, 1991).

II. Outcomes Assessment in the I-P-O Model

In the language of systems theory, a researcher might ask the following question: having processed basic raw materials (students), what are the tangible products or outputs of a college or university? Are the products relevant to the society in which the institution functions? Do they exhibit an inherent quality that merits continued support for the institution? In years past, it was simply assumed that postsecondary institutions operated in the public interest. Colleges and universities were left on their own to decide what students, and implicitly the larger society, needed. This is no longer the case. The push for assessment challenges colleges not only to demonstrate that students are learning, but also that the curricula and faculty scholarship are characterized by quality. As in other aspects of assessment, institutional research can play a central role.

Clearly, a primary student output is graduates (especially for four-year institutions). Institutional research offices traditionally produce reports both for internal and external consumption (e.g., IPEDS Survey of Completions), which display the number of individuals in a given department or discipline who are awarded associates, bachelors, masters, and doctoral degrees.

While such reports are important, they do not speak to the "quality" of the graduate. A traditional measure of how viable an institution's graduates are is the post-graduation activity of those individuals. Are they securing jobs? Are the jobs curriculum related? Who are the major employers? Which graduate or post-two year schools are being attended? How many graduates are attending medical or law school and what is the caliber of these postgraduate institutions?

These and similar questions are the focus of follow-up studies, nearly universally administered by institutional research offices during the 12 months following graduation. Appendix 7 provides an example of a post-graduation survey than can be utilized to help answer these questions. This type of survey is usually administered to all academic year degree recipients (e.g., associate, bachelors, masters, and/or doctoral level), with a follow-up mailing to nonrespondents at 4-6 weeks. As well, this survey can be generated directly from the computerized Student Records System. A program can be designed to extract all relevant records information on graduates (degrees earned, major, cumulative grade point average, gender, ethnicity, and so on). This data file is then merged to the survey responses. As a time saver, the program which generates the database can also write the questionnaire onto a mainframe printer, and pre-print the address and degree information shown in Appendix 7.

Note, however, that this survey is helpful in describing the *immediate* post-graduation plans of students. Many institutional research offices systematically contact alumni at regular intervals to update career and educational information over the years. For example, it is possible to schedule alumni surveys at 5 year intervals. This enables the institutional researcher to collect data on individuals who change careers, attend graduate school later, or complete graduate degree requirements. It also allows graduates more time to reflect on their previous educational experience.

Commercial vendors such as ACT, and the College Board also produce a broad array of Alumni Surveys, Career Planning Surveys, and other instruments for assessing the student "products" of an institution. These may or may not be appropriate for a specific college or university; a questionnaire or survey prepared in-house may be more suited to specific information needs. In either instance, the information collected can and should serve as a basis for evaluating current activity at the institution, and for developing appropriate policy recommendations.

Some institutional research offices are now engaged in other types of alumni follow-up studies. While post-graduation placement data one to five years after college are an important component of outcomes analysis, it is also possible to obtain an even more detailed picture of the college or university experience.

Colleges and universities may wish to know answers to questions such as: To what extent is the curriculum studied during college relevant to activity in the workplace? How successful is the graduate as measured by promotions and salary increases. To what extent did the college experience enhance the individual's awareness of social issues? Prepare him/her to become fully involved in community life? Heighten awareness of cultural/aesthetic issues? These, and other "value added" dimensions of the college experience are being included in systematic assessment of how the educational enterprise affects students.

One of the national leaders in alumni survey research is Gerlinda Melchiori. Newcomers and other institutional researchers will profit by obtaining copies of her work in the *New Directions for Institutional Research* series, *Alumni Research: Methods and Applications* (1989). Jossey-Bass, Inc.

Another useful article summarizing good information for developing employer surveys is presented by Trudy Banta (1993), Critique of a method for surveying employers. *AIR Professional File, No. 47,* Association for Institutional Research.

Institutional Research Offices have also developed "Employer Surveys" for selected professional programs to determine the extent to which "consumers" of University graduates are satisfied with the product. Programs such as Nursing, Business and Economics, and Equine Science want to know if and how their graduates are prepared for their fields. Results from these surveys are then addressed in curricula for current students.

III. Institution and Personnel Assessment

In addition to assessing students, some institutional researchers are involved in strategic planning for the institution and/or assessing various programs or aspects of the campus. Listed below are some of the possible programs or service areas that may be included in the institutional or personnel assessment program:

> Campus Climate Studies
> Prospective Student Programs
> Department and Program Evaluation
> Strategic / Long-term Planning
> Student Satisfaction with the College Environment
> Employee Satisfaction and Quality of Life Surveys
> Focus Group Meetings
> Employee Salary Equity Studies (Internal and External Comparators)
> Faculty and Administrator Productivity Analyses

A. Assessing Programs, Services, or the Campus Environment

Because of tight budgets, limited staffs, or lack of technical expertise, colleagues in other offices on campus may look to the institutional research office for help in program evaluation. Examples include evaluations of new student orientations, preview programs for prospective students, evaluating curricular needs, and satisfaction of faculty, professional, and support staff. The Evaluation of New Student Orientation and The Campus Community Scale are two relevant examples of how institutional research can be a substantial resource for campus research.

1. Evaluation of New Student Orientation - Many administrators responsible for conducting student support programs need to know that current efforts are worth supporting in the future or what areas of the program may

require improvement. Often, institutional researchers work with the Orientation staff at institution to develop an instrument to evaluate the New Student Orientation (NSO) program. Because this is a locally-produced instrument, it is relatively inexpensive and can be modified for each administration as needed. In a collaborative approach to data collection, Orientation staff may distribute and collect the survey at NSO and then send it to the Institutional Research Office for data entry and analysis. A brief summary report can then submitted to the director of NSO by the institutional researcher.

2. Campus Community Scale (CCS). Many institutions have taken on a renewed interest in studying the campus climate and its effects upon students. Astin (1993), Noel, Levitz and Saluri (1985), among others, discuss the need for a friendly campus climate and the benefits of good student-environment fit. A recently developed survey, the Campus Community Scale is based upon Boyer's (1990) six principles that are essential for an effective college campus.

The thirty-six items on the CSS questionnaire can offer the institutional researcher an assessment of how caring, just, open, disciplined, purposeful, and celebrative students believe their campus is. Findings from a climate survey such as the CCS can help institutional researchers determine which areas or programs may need to be implemented or modified in order to better serve students. In addition, information from such a survey can help begin to explain why attrition among certain groups of students may be occurring at higher than average rates. For more information, contact Dr. Steven Janosik, 1106 Mourning Dove Drive, Blacksburg, VA 24060.

B. Faculty and Staff Measures

In addition to measures of students or programs within the institution, institutional researchers are often charged with collecting attitudinal data or measures of faculty or non-teaching staff growth as well as on-going inventories or other measures of productivity. The following may be pertinent questions: What 'quality of life' issues are most important to faculty at this time? How many students can each faculty member effectively advise? How many patents are derived from pure and applied research on campus? How many copyrights are issued for books and other publications authored by faculty and staff? How many articles appear annually in refereed scholarly journals? How extensively do faculty and other personnel consult with governmental agencies and industry?

Some information to answer these questions may be available within the institution's personnel data base. Faculty growth, for example, can be (indirectly) assessed by examining such measures as academic rank, years in rank, years in service to the institution, and merit salary increases. Non-teaching personnel can similarly be analyzed by looking at job title, years in title, promotions, and merit salary increases. These data provide rudimentary measures of personnel development, but do not really offer details of the activities which underpin the growth.

These and other measures of satisfaction and productivity are equally as important as student attitudes and cognitive gains. The attitudinal and productivity measures related to faculty are empirically quantifiable, and will be discussed in greater length in Chapter Five.

In addition to effort analyses, many institutions administer quality of life surveys to personnel to assess satisfaction with working environment, opportunities for professional growth and development, career path/promotion opportunities, and with monetary and non-monetary rewards systems. These instruments can be purchased or prepared locally. Structured much like a student satisfaction survey, but with a different focus, the surveys can be useful in isolating sources of employee dissatisfaction before they become major labor relations problems.

The Cooperative Institutional Research Program offers an interesting Faculty Quality of Life Survey. This instrument provides well-developed questions along a wide array of faculty issues as well as comparative norms for two and four-year public and private institutions. For more information, contact the CIRP at the address mentioned in Chapter 2.

Broad (and brief) surveys of satisfaction for professionals and support staff can be developed with input of individuals from that constituency. A survey of support staff, such as shown in Appendix 8, can be easily completed anonymously by staff, then sent to the institutional research office for analysis.

Summary

Although the level of participation will certainly vary from school to school, most institutional researchers are involved in one or more assessment projects during the course of the academic year. Whether these projects involve measures of student academic or personal growth, levels of faculty or staff satisfaction, or development of a comprehensive strategic plan for your institution, your skills in this areas are likely to be used and sharpened. Methods and measures used in an assessment projects may well fit into more than one component of the I-P-O model or may serve dual purposes. For example, while assessing the campus climate might be intended as an evaluation of the process for one institution, it may be intended as an outcome evaluation for another. Assessment will certainly remain an important issue that most institutional researchers will encounter. There are many helpful resources available, a few of which have been presented in this Chapter.

CHAPTER FIVE: FINANCES

In recent years, and most especially since the advent of difficult economic times for higher education in the late 1980s and the early of the 1990s, institutional researchers have increasingly been asked to provide analytical support in assessing the fiscal health of colleges and universities. This chapter provides institutional researchers who do not have formal business training some basic insight on how to approach financial analyses.

There are a number of excellent books that describe the major financial issues confronting American higher education today. A particularly clear and lucid volume is *The Economics of American Universities*, edited by Stephen A. Hoenack and Eileen L. Collins (Albany, New York: State University of New York Press, 1990). The book gives a thorough theoretical treatment to the overall concept of higher education finances, but is particularly strong in its discussions of cost functions and strategies for assessing them at a college or university.

In providing analytical financial data, the institutional researcher will likely be asked what it costs to educate a humanities major compared with a major in life or physical sciences; or what it costs to deliver a student credit hour of instruction in the fine arts compared with engineering. Similarly, institutional researchers are increasingly being asked to develop strategies for assessing administrative costs and efficiencies. The Hoenack and Collins volume provides solid theoretical grounding in these areas. And while the title of the volume refers to the economics of American universities, the chapters are applicable to the full range of higher education institutions: from research universities to two-year community colleges.

While a firm theoretical grounding in the finances of higher education is helpful, ultimately the institutional researcher/policy analyst has to move from theory to practice. The remainder of this chapter will focus on practical strategies for examining institutional finances. A useful starting point is to examine financial documents which describe in general terms how the institution operates. Virtually every college and university in the country uses a specialized type of accounting referred to as "fund accounting." Consistent with that practice, institutions annually generate a "Statement of Current Funds Revenues, Expenditures, and Other Changes," often abbreviated to "Current Funds Statement." This statement can be found in an institution's Annual

INSTITUTION X
Statements of Current Funds Revenues, Expenditures, Transfers, and Changes in Fund Balances

(Thousands of Dollars)

Year Ended June 30, 199_

Line No.			Unrestricted	Restricted	Total
	Revenues				
1	Tuition and Fees	$	121,693	--	121,693
	Government Appropriations:				
2	State		61,394	6,723	68,117
3	Federal		40	2,979	3,019
	Contracts and Grants:				
4	State		1,087	5,391	6,478
5	Federal		5,273	23,607	28,880
6	Other		1,232	5,539	6,771
7	Gifts		435	8,566	9,001
8	Endowments		18,278	3,855	22,133
9	Temporary Investments		5,328	440	5,768
10	Activities of educational departments		3,801	--	3,801
	Other sources:				
11	User service charges		3,782	--	3,782
12	Campus conferences		3,391	--	3,391
13	Miscellaneous		4,422	1	4,423
14	Auxiliary operations		50,151	--	50,151
15	Total Revenues	$	280,307	57,101	337,408

65

INSTITUTION X

Statements of Current Funds Revenues, Expenditures, Transfers, and Changes in Fund Balances

(Thousands of Dollars)

Year Ended June 30, 199_

Line No.		Unrestricted	Restricted	Total
	Expenditures, transfers, and changes in fund balances:			
	Educational and general:			
16	Instruction and departmental research	$ 111,997	10,524	122,521
17	Sponsored resesarch	5,562	28,784	34,346
18	Extension and public service	7,348	4,891	12,239
19	Academic support	16,651	785	17,436
20	Primary programs	141,558	44.984	186,542
21	Student services	9,920	307	10,227
22	Operations and maintenance of plant	17,472	184	17,656
23	General institutional support	25,914	400	26,314
24	Support programs	53,306	891	54,197
25	Student aid	12,614	8,965	21,579
26	Subtotal expenditures	207,478	54,850	262,318
	Mandatory transfers to other funds:			
27	Principal and interest	2,320	17	2,337
28	Loan funds and matching grants	22	--	22
	Other transfers to other funds:			
29	Restricted funds	94	(94)	--
30	Loan funds	(1)	--	(1)
31	Endowment and similar funds	698	1,225	1,923
32	Unexpended plant funds	13,626	102	13,728
33	Renewal and replacement funds	5,322	--	5,322
34	Retirement of indebtedness	80	--	80
	Changes in fund balances:			
35	Allocations to current funds	12,417	--	12,417
36	Allocations from current funds	(9,559)	--	(9,559)
37	Changes in restricted fund balances	--	995	995
38	Transfers and allocations	25,019	2,245	27,264
39	Total educational and general	$ 232,497	57,085	289,582

INSTITUTION X

Statements of Current Funds Revenues, Expenditures, Transfers, and Changes in Fund Balances

(Thousands of Dollars)

Year Ended June 30, 199_

Line No.		Unrestricted	Restricted	Total
	Auxiliary operations:			
40	Expenditures	$ 40,432	16	40,448
	Mandatory transfers to other funds:			
41	Principal and interest	3,174	--	3,174
	Other transfers to other funds:			
42	Unexpended plant funds	68	--	68
43	Renewwal and replacement funds	4,256	--	4,256
	Changes in fund balances:			
44	Allocations to current funds	(120)	--	(120)
45	Total auxiliary operations	$ 47,810	16	47,826
46	Total current funds expenditures, transfers and changes in fund balances	$ 280,307	57,101	337,408

Financial Report, and data extracted from the Current Funds Statement also appear on the annual IPEDS Survey of Institutional Finances.

A sample of an actual Current Funds Statement from one institution is shown in Table 5.1. Essentially, this document identifies revenue sources and expenditure categories for funds available at the institution throughout the fiscal year.

Revenues include funds brought into the institution from tuition and fees, governmental appropriations, contracts and grants, gifts, income from endowment, income from temporary investments, revenue from other education-related sources, and from auxiliary operations. Auxiliary operations are those self-supporting entities such as dining halls, residence halls, and bookstores, which enhance the institution but which are not essential to the central mission of a college or university, i.e., teaching, research, and public service.

Expenditures, on the other hand, refer to moneys from current funds that are spent on primary functions: instruction, sponsored research, extension and public service, and academic support, as well as on general support functions such as student services, operation and maintenance of the physical plant, and institutional support (euphemistically referred to as "administration"). Expenditures on student aid are also reported here.

In addition to revenues and expenditures, the statement also reports transfers of funds between current funds and other fund types (e.g., loan funds, endowment funds, plant funds, etc.). Some of these transfers are mandatory, that is, they are legally required by statute, regulation or trustee resolution. These include payment of principal and interest on bond indebtedness, as well as loan funds and matching grants. The institution also has the option for non-mandatory transfers and allocations, which include moving moneys from current funds to other fund types when revenues exceed expenditures, or moving moneys in the other direction when a deficit or other need situation occurs. Mandatory and non-mandatory transfers and allocations, respectively, are clearly identified on the statement.

The Current Funds Statement characteristically groups funds into "unrestricted" (i.e., can be used for any purpose by the institution) and "restricted" (can be used only for the purpose stipulated by the revenue source). For purposes of discussion in this chapter, discussion will focus on the total funds column in the example statement.

The first step in analyzing the Current Funds Statement is identification of what are referred to as "Education and General Revenues," "Education and General Expenditures," and "Mandatory and Non-Mandatory Transfers, Allocations, and Other Changes." The notion of "Education and General" (E&G) refers to the cost of doing business that is central to the institutional mission of teaching, research, and service. Thus, E&G revenues embrace all current fund revenues except those from auxiliary operations, hospitals, and independent operations. Table 5.1 shows that total E&G revenues for the fiscal year can be derived by taking Total revenues (Line 15: $337,400,000) and subtracting Auxiliary Operations (Line 14: $50,151,000) to arrive at an E&G revenue figure of $287,249,000.

E&G expenditures (Line 26: $262,318,000) is comprised of all current fund expenditures on primary functions (Line 20: $186,542,000), support functions (Line 24: $54,197,000), and student aid (Line 25: $21,579,000). E&G mandatory transfers, $2,359,000, is the sum of Lines 27 and 28, while E&G non-mandatory transfers and allocations, $24,905,000, is the sum of Lines 29 through 37.

Total revenues, $337,408,000, are the sum of E&G revenues plus revenues from auxiliary operations. When total E&G expenditures, transfers and allocations (Line 39, $289,582,000) are added to expenditures, transfers and allocations in auxiliary operations (Line 45, $47,826,000) the sum, $337,408,000, is equal to total revenues, indicating a balanced budget. Most institutions are required to close out the fiscal year with a budget in balance, and it is generally after examining revenues and expenditures, that transfers, allocations, and other changes bring about the necessary fine tuning to achieve balance.

With a rudimentary understanding of the data elements contained in the Current Funds Statement, the institutional researcher can generate a substantial amount of useful information that will assist senior planners in charting the institution's financial course. For example, it is helpful to look at growth patterns over time in E&G revenues and E&G expenditures and mandatory transfers. (Mandatory transfers are usually folded in with expenditures, as they are funds which must be transferred to specific uses and are not available for discretionary use by the institution. In other words, they are as good as spent.)

Consider the trend data shown in Table 5.2. By focusing on E&G revenues, and E&G expenditures and mandatory transfers, the analysis is centered on those funds related to institutional mission, i.e., those moneys raised for and spent on teaching, research, and public service. In each of the fiscal years shown in the table, E&G revenues exceed E&G expenditures and mandatory transfers. However, the table also indicates that the rate of growth for E&G revenues and mandatory transfers is greater than that for E&G revenues. This is a warning signal that, unabated, the current trend will jeopardize the institution's fiscal health in the not too distant future. Keep in mind that these are actual data from a real institution, and tables of this sort can galvanize the attention of the campus community toward understanding the financial climate and supporting appropriate policy action to restore the growth rate to a more appropriate balance.

Ratio Analysis

Similarly, useful information about how an institution obtains its funding and how it uses those funds can also be extracted from the Current Funds Statement. The analytic tool of choice in this process is referred to as "ratio analysis." A series of "Revenue Contribution Ratios" and "Expenditure Demand Ratios" can be calculated from the Statement of Revenues, Expenditures, and Other Changes. Revenue contribution ratios measure the relative contribution of each of the major revenue streams to the expenditure functions that they are expected to cover. Conversely, the expenditure allocation ratios measure the demand from each of the major expenditure functions on education and general revenues.

Examples of revenue contribution ratios would be those for "tuition and fees" and for "state appropriation." In each instance, the respective revenue stream is divided by "E&G Expenditures and Mandatory Transfers." Looking again at the Current Funds Statement in Table 5.1, the Tuition Contribution Ratio is 0.460. This reflects tuition revenue (Line 1: $121,693,000) divided by E&G expenditures and mandatory transfers ($264,677,000, the sum of Lines 26,27, and 28). This suggests that 46% of the costs of teaching, research, and service at the institution could be supported by revenues from tuition and fees. The Tuition Contribution Ratio will tend to be lower at state-supported institutions, and will be higher at private or church-related institutions. This particular ratio is a good measure of the relative tuition dependency of the college or university.

A State Appropriation Contribution Ratio is similarly calculated by dividing state appropriation (Line 2: $68,117,000) by E&G Expenditures and Mandatory Transfers. The resulting ratio, 0.257, suggests that 25.7% of the costs of teaching, research, and service could be supported by revenue from state appropriation. Again, one would look for a relationship between the Tuition Contribution Ratio and the State Appropriation Contribution ratio at publicly supported four-year and two-year schools, with the state appropriation compensating for the lower tuition ratio.

The reader who wishes to pursue the principles of fund accounting and ratio analysis in more detail is referred to the following excellent sources:

NACUBO, KMPG Peat Marwick. (1990). *Financial Accounting and Reporting Manual for Higher Education*. Washington, D.C.: National Association of College and University Business Officers.

This is the college/university accounting bible. A multi-volume set, it is expensive and is a source that the institutional researcher will use only from time to time. Chances are, it is already on the shelf in the business office; better to borrow it than buy it.

Minter J., Hughes, K.S., Robinson, D.D., Turk, F.J., Buchanan, A.D., & Prager, F.J. (1987). *Ratio Analysis in Higher Education*. New York: Peat Marwick & Main Co.

This volume describes how ratio analysis can be used to assess institutional financial health, and how ratio analysis can be extended to interinstitutional comparisons to determine the position of a specific institution against those of several peers. Clearly written for the newcomer to higher education finance, and inexpensive to purchase, the manual is particularly useful when trying to compare expenditure patterns at a given institution, as evidenced by expenditure demand ratios, with comparable patterns at selected comparator schools. Explanations for variations in expenditure patterns can be hypothesized by looking at dependency upon alternative revenue streams as evidenced by revenue contribution ratios.

Expenditure demand ratios are similar in concept. Total E&G revenues in the Current Funds Statement were previously calculated at $287,249,000. This figure becomes the denominator in demand ratios, which show how much of E&G revenues might be consumed by major expenditure categories. For example, looking at the Current Funds Statement, Instruction and Departmental Research (Line 16, $122,521,000), when divided by total E&G revenues, results in a ratio of 0.427, suggesting that this particular function consumes 42.7% of total institutional current funds revenues.

71

Table 5.2:

Comparison of Growth Rate in E & G Revenues Compared with
E & G Expenditures and Mandatory Transfers:
FY 1983 through FY 1993 (Dollars in Millions)

	FY 1983	FY 1985	FY 1987	FY 1989	FY 1991	FY 1993
E&G Revenues	$137,696	$161,309	$193,030	$228,199	$270,124	$299,278
% Increase over FY 1983	–	17.1	40.2	65.7	92.2	117.3
E&G Expenditures and Mandatory Transfers	$126,371	$144,493	$177,517	$221,766	$255,519	$277,575
% Increase over FY 1983	–	14.3	40.5	75.5	102.2	119.7

Ratio analysis is particularly instructive when examining revenue and expenditure patterns over a multiple year time frame. While one might well be concerned about the absolute dollar increase in revenues from tuition or state appropriation, as evidenced in the Current Funds Statement for a given fiscal year, the extent to which an institution has become more or less tuition dependent, or the extent to which non-instructional functions are eroding investment in the classroom, are of substantial concern for planning and policy purposes. These trends can be examined through longitudinal ratio analyses.

Interinstitutional Financial Data

In looking at interinstitutional data, John Minter Associates produce a series of volumes annually, including *Management Ratios* and *Financial Statistics and Ratios*. These volumes extend the foregoing discussion of ratio analysis, and display revenue contribution ratios, expenditure demand ratios, and a number of other ratios dealing with issues such as physical plant assets and endowment. Minter provides these ratios for virtually every four-year and two-year college and university in the nation. Culled from the National Center for Educational Statistics' (NCES) Integrated Postsecondary Education Data System (IPEDS) annual surveys, the data are arrayed by institution and by Carnegie classification. They are very useful resources, and information concerning price and availability can be obtained from:

John Minter Associates
2400 Central Avenue, Suite B-2
Boulder, Colorado 80301

Another useful comparative resource is the series of volumes on higher education finance produced by Research Associates of Washington, D.C., under the leadership of Kent Halstead. Halstead's cornerstone volume is *Higher Education Revenues and Expenditures: A Study of Institutional Costs*. Basic factors that drive the cost of higher education, particularly as they relate to common revenue and expenditure categories, are discussed in clear, understandable language. Strategies for conducting interinstitutional comparisons with respect to revenues, by type, per FTE student enrolled, and expenditures, by type, per FTE student are presented. Halstead pays particular attention to criteria for selecting appropriate peer groups for economic comparisons, and discusses such issues as geographic price differentials and economies of scale when examining interinstitutional data.

73

Research Associates annually produces a companion volume titled *Institutional Data* which examines the basic revenue and expenditure data/FTE student, as developed in *A Study of Institutional Costs*, and extracted from the NCES/IPEDS surveys for virtually every two-year and four-year college and university in the nation. When used in conjunction with the Minter Associates' volumes on ratio analysis, a robust picture of the relative fiscal health of an institution emerges, especially as it relates to specific peers.

Research Associates of Washington also annually produces a volume titled *Inflation Measures for Schools and Colleges.* The volume tracks inflationary pressure on specific higher education price drivers including faculty and professional salaries, library materials, general supplies and expense, and capital costs. These price drivers are then related to increases in tuition, room, and board. Research Associates argue that the Consumer Price Index (CPI), as a measure of inflation, does not adequately describe higher education, where prices tend to increase at levels more rapid than the general economy. They have developed the Higher Education Price Index (HEPI), which they describe in detail, and use as a benchmark in conjunction with the CPI for assessing inflationary pressures on higher education. Colleges and universities analyzing tuition increases over time, faculty salary patterns, and growth patterns in other higher education cost drivers will find this volume helpful.

Those wishing to learn more about resources available from Research Associates should contact that group at the following address:

Research Associates of Washington
2605 Klingle Road NW
Washington, D.C. 20008

Other external financial data resources of value to the institutional researcher include the following:

1. *Student Charges at Public, Four Year Institutions.* Compiled jointly by the American Association of State Colleges and Universities (AASCU) and the National Association of State Universities and Land Grant Colleges (NASULGC), this annual publication lists resident and non-resident tuition and room and board rates at member institutions for undergraduate and graduate students, respectively. Data are presented for the current and prior year, and provide a means of comparing the growth in student charges at a given, publicly supported institution against that of AASCU/NASULGC peers.

Contact: Office of Association Research
           American Association of State Colleges and Universities
           One Dupont Circle NW, Suite 700
           Washington, DC 20036

2. *The College Cost Book.* Published by the College Board using data from their Annual Survey of Colleges, this volume provides information on student expenses at both public and private institutions, by state. However, unlike the AASCU/NASULGC volume which report current academic year data, *The College Cost Book* reports information that is a year old, and is of less value in timely benchmarking studies.

Contact: College Board
           Publication Orders
           Box 886
           New York, NY 10101

3. *Voluntary Support for Higher Education.* Most higher education institutions have placed increased emphasis on development/fund-raising activity. This volume, produced by the Council for Aid to Education (CAE) provides comparative data on fund-raising measures for over 1000 colleges and universities nationally. The publication reports comparative statistics on such measures as total voluntary support, corporate support, alumni support, unrestricted giving, gifts of property, etc. The report does not include endowment income or income from other investments, nor does it report governmental appropriations.

Contact: Council for Aid to Education, Inc.
           51 Madison Avenue
           New York, NY 10010

4. *Comparative Financial Statistics for Public Two Year Colleges.* Compiled annually, this volume provides comparative fiscal data for a national sample of public two year colleges. Extracted from the IPEDS Survey of Institutional Finances, and supplemented by data from member institutions of the National Association of College and University Business Officers (NACUBO), the report provides two-year college benchmarks for revenues, expenditures, staffing ratios, etc.

Contact: NACUBO Center for Institutional Accounting, Finance,
and Management
One Dupont Circle, NW, Suite 500
Washington, DC 20036

Salary and Compensation Comparisons

Examining institutional finances at any college or university quickly reveals that the major expenditures are salaries, benefits, and other employment costs. Education is a personnel intensive operation, and costs associated with attracting and retaining employees are the single largest expenditure category. It is therefore essential that colleges and universities monitor salary practices to ensure optimal utilization of personnel funds. Institutional researchers are frequently called upon to assist in this process, usually in two areas - analysis of salaries with respect to external market competitiveness and analysis of salaries with respect to internal equity.

In determining external market competitiveness, it is useful to identify a cadre of peer institutions who reflect comparable academic programs with the focal institution, and which also reflect comparable cost of living characteristics. The publications from John Minter Associates and from Research Associates of Washington referenced earlier in this chapter provide strategies for identifying peer groups of institutions. The National Center for Higher Education Management Systems (NCHEMS), referenced in Chapter 2, provide peer identification services for a fee.

Once a peer group is established, it is then possible to use a variety of sources in examining external market competitiveness with respect to compensation. Included among those resources are the following:

1. The Annual Report on the Economic Status of the Profession. The annual March/April issue of *Academe*, the Bulletin of the American Association of University Professors is entirely devoted to analysis of faculty salaries at all colleges and universities participating in the AAUP Survey of Faculty Compensation. Data are provided at the aggregate level which show average faculty salary and compensation by rank, for national and regional norms, by institution type (doctoral, comprehensive, general baccalaureate, two year) and by institutional control (public, private, and church-related). In addition to normative data, the volume provides average salary and total compensation (salary plus comparable benefits), by rank, for each individual institution in the study. Data are also provided with respect to tenure rates and gender of faculty. This is a rich data base that enables solid market comparisons at the institutional

76

level for virtually any college or university in the country. The data on total compensation, and benefits as a percentage of salary, are particularly instructive. As noted, the data reflect institutional aggregations and do not provide detail at the department/discipline level.

Contact: AAUP
            Suite 500, 1012 14th Street, NW
            Washington, DC 20005

2. The Office of Institutional Research at Oklahoma State University annually conducts a survey of faculty salaries, by rank and by academic discipline at institutions belonging to the National Association of State Universities and Land Grant Colleges (NASULGC). The Oklahoma Salary Survey provides data by academic rank, aggregated at the national and regional level, for a broad spectrum of academic disciplines. These statistics enable the researcher to discern salary levels in high priced disciplines such as business and engineering, contrasted with lesser paid disciplines, e.g. fine arts and humanities. The analyses are performed at the programmatic level within disciplines, and it is possible to look at comparative salaries for accounting, chemical engineering, philosophy, and art, as examples. These data also include average salaries for new assistant professors, which provide a valuable benchmark for looking at salary compression (i.e., new assistant professors being paid at levels comparable to or exceeding associate professors). Note that the Oklahoma Survey information focuses exclusively on salary and does not address total compensation. These data provide aggregated benchmarks and do not identify specific institutions, unlike the AAUP analysis.

Contact: Office of Institutional Research
            Oklahoma State University
            Whitehurst Hall 301
            Stillwater, OK   74078

3. The College and University Personnel Association (CUPA), working in conjunction with Appalachian State University, have modified the Oklahoma Salary Survey methodology to include private institutions and non-NASULGC public institutions. The difference from Oklahoma Salary Survey methodology relate primarily to discipline groupings. CUPA also conducts an Annual Survey of Administrative Compensation, examining salaries of senior administrators from president /chief executive officer down to deans and directors of major administrative units. For both the CUPA Faculty Salary Survey and the Survey of Administrative Compensation, participating institutions may request special analyses for a fee which aggregate the data from

a pool of specifically identified peer institutions. The only requirement is that the peer institutions that are requested must also have participated in the study. Also, the institutions in the special analysis are not identified but kept completely anonymous.

Contact: College and University Personnel Association
1233 20th Street, NW, Suite 301
Washington, DC   20036

Salary Equity Analyses

Studies of external market competitiveness of salaries and compensation levels require a set of peer institutions with which to compare faculty at the home institution. Salary equity analyses, on the other hand, focus on fair and equitable compensation *within* a given institution. Traditional salary equity studies focused upon gender, and usually employed regression analysis of male salaries using predictor variables such as highest degree earned and years of experience, to estimate the comparable salary level for a female with a similar demographic profile. Recent court cases have suggested that the concept of equity be more broadly based to ensure that compensation is equitable for both men and women.

The approaches to salary equity analyses are varied, and constitute a body of literature unto themselves. Institutional researchers faced with this type of compensation analysis are directed to the following references for developing a strategic approach to this type of study:

McCabe, G. (1979). The interpretation of regression analysis results in sex and race discrimination problems. *Proceedings of the Social Statistics Section, American Statistical Association*, 27-29.

Gray, M.W. & Scott, E.L. (May, 1980). A statistical remedy for statistically identified discrimination. *Academe*, 174-181.

McLaughlin, G.W., Zirkes, M.B., & Mahan, B.T. (1983). Multicollinearity and testing questions in sex equity. *Research in Higher Education, 19* (3), 277-283.

Multiple regression is still the most widely used tool in equity analysis, and these three references will provide a road map into both the analysis and the literature. Alternative approaches to equity analysis are emerging, however, and the following references are of interest:

Braskamp, L.A. & Johnson, D.R. (1978). The use of a parity-equity model to evaluate faculty salary policies. *Research in Higher Education*, *8*, 57-66.

Bereman, N.A. & Scott, J.A. (1991). Using the compa-ratio to detect gender bias in faculty salaries. *Journal of Higher Education*, *62* (5), 556-569.

As noted earlier, litigation and court decisions are very much a part of the compensation process. Within that context, a valuable resource has emerged which should find a place on the shelves of most institutional research offices. Joseph L. Gastwirth has written a two volume work, *Statistical Reasoning in Law and Public Policy*, (New York: Academic Press/Harcourt Brace Jovanovich, Publishers, 1988) which details legal decisions with respect to the use of various statistical approaches to salary equity analysis, as well as other areas of public policy studies.

This chapter has provided a broad overview of ways in which institutional research can provide assistance is assessing the economy and efficiency with which institutional resources are acquired and expended. This discussion is certainly not exhaustive. The reader is urged to pursue the resources referenced in this chapter, and more important, to cultivate solid working relationships with colleagues in the business office on campus.

CHAPTER SIX:
COST AND PRODUCTIVITY STUDIES

Chapter Five underscored the necessity for careful management of fiscal resources during difficult economic times for higher education. If fiscal resources are to be conserved, human resources are equally important. This is true for all institutions of higher education, two-year community college to doctoral level research universities. This chapter discusses productivity in higher education, i.e., managing human resources in a manner that ensures a maximum return on investment.

Before approaching the issue of productivity, the institutional researcher would be well served to read relevant articles which have shaped the debate on the subject. Robert Zemsky of the University of Pennsylvania and William Massy of Stanford University attracted national attention in recent years with their concept of the "academic ratchet and administrative lattice." Essentially, they argue that faculty have generally developed stronger allegiances to their academic disciplines than to the institutions that employ them. Because institutions value and reward those individuals who attract external funding for research and service, faculty have developed entrepreneurial instincts for attracting those external funds, often at the expense of undergraduate teaching.

Zemsky and Massy further argue that where faculty do teach, the course content tends to be in the area of their specialization, with introductory and general curriculum courses left to part-time faculty and graduate teaching assistants. Finally, the authors contend that the shift in faculty activity away from teaching and toward those activities that ensure tenure and salary increases has resulted in a proliferation of administrative positions to assume responsibilities formerly belonging to faculty, ranging from student advising to administering sponsored programs. As a result, a college education costs more, faculty are teaching less, and general public satisfaction with colleges and universities is at an all time low.

Whether or not one agrees with the "ratchet and lattice" concept, or the various other critiques of productivity in American higher education, it is important to be versed in the underlying concepts. These issues are the focus of debate in state education departments, state legislatures, and among consumer groups as the cost of higher education, and continued willingness to pay for it, comes under close scrutiny.

The following references should prove helpful in acquiring initial familiarity with the issues:

Alfred, R.L. & Weissman, J. (1987). *Higher Education and the Public Trust.* Washington, DC: ERIC Clearinghouse on Higher Education/Association for the Study of Higher Education.

Langtitt, T.W. (1990). The cost of higher education: lessons learned from the health care industry. *Change, 22* (6), 8-15.

Massy, W.F. & Zemsky, R. (1994). Faculty discretionary time: departments and the academic ratchet. *The Journal of Higher Education, 65* (1), 1-22.

Rosovsky, H. (1992). Excerpts from Annual Report of the Dean of the Faculty of Arts and Science at Harvard University, 1990-91. *Policy Perspectives, 4* (3).

Zemsky, R. & Massy, W.F. (1990). Cost containment. *Change, 22* (6), 16-22.

While these references provide useful background information on the issue of productivity, the researcher should also have some theoretical grounding in the literature on cost and productivity as well. There are two volumes which arguably should be on the reference shelf of any institutional research office engaged in productivity analyses:

Hoenack, S.A. & Collins, E.L. (Eds.). (1990). *The Economics of American Universities.* Albany, New York: State University of New York Press.

The reader is particularly directed to two chapters in this volume, Stephen Hoenack's, "An Economist's Perspective On Costs Within Higher Education Institutions," and Paul Brinkman's, "Higher Education Cost Functions."

Hollins, C.S. (Ed.). (1992). *Containing Costs and Improving Productivity in Higher Education*. In *New Directions for Institutional Research, (No. 75)*. San Francisco: Jossey-Bass, Inc.

This volume is written to provide pragmatic background information for the institutional researcher about to embark on cost and productivity analyses. It is a excellent volume of practical information. For a particularly useful "how to" discussion of analytical strategies, the reader is directed to the chapter by Michael Middaugh and David Hollowell, Examining Academic and Administrative Productivity Measures.

General Considerations

What are some of the general concerns in analyzing cost and productivity in higher education? Arriving at consistent definitions with respect to what we mean by "cost" and "productivity" is an important first step. Suppose an institutional researcher were asked what it costs to deliver a single student credit hour of instruction in Chemistry during a given fiscal year. Or what it costs, on average, to process an admissions application or to complete registration procedures for a typical student. Colleges and university accounting systems generally collect enough information to answer these questions, but do not necessarily store it in a fashion where it is easily retrieved. For example, any institution completing the IPEDS Annual Survey of Institutional Finances supplies data for total direct expenditures for "instruction" and for "general institutional support." It would seem logical that in developing the IPEDS survey amount for "instruction," expenditures for the Chemistry Department and all of the other units on campus involved in instruction would be aggregated upward to an institutional total.

The same might be argued for the Registrar's office and other appropriate administrative units in arriving at a total "institutional support" number. Then one should be able to disaggregate to arrive at the unit costs. Although this is a good theory, it is a difficult practice. Institutional budgeting among organizational units does not necessarily coincide with discrete academic curricula and administrative functions. Multiple academic programs can be housed in a single department. That is, a small college might have a "Department of Physical Sciences" which houses faculty who teach physics, chemistry, and earth sciences. Similarly, administrative functions are frequently combined in a single office (e.g., Office of Admissions and Financial Aid or Office of College Development and Alumni Affairs). Assessment of unit costs and productivity quickly becomes a complex matter.

Cost questions become even more murky when the concept of total cost is introduced. The example above talks about direct expenditures in looking at instruction. Certainly faculty and departmental salaries and support budgets can be charged directly to the cost of delivering a student credit hour of instruction in that department. But what of indirect costs? How does one estimate the cost of lighting and heating classroom and laboratory space used by the department? What is the department's share of the cost of operating the library which is used by its students and those of other departments? How does one pass along the cost of recruiting, admitting, and registering students to the departments in which they enroll? Or the cost of securing and administering external contracts and grants? Or operating a campus public safety unit?

Kent Halstead, of Research Associates of Washington, has written extensively on higher education costs. He has developed a formula for full instructional cost, estimated as "the sum of direct expenditures for instruction and student services plus prorated indirect costs. The indirect costs equal total academic and institutional support and operation and maintenance of plant less overhead for funded research and public service estimated at 30 percent of the expenditures for these two functions." This is a general approximation of full cost that may be appropriate for broad interinstitutional comparisons. Unfortunately, this formula lacks precision for use at the level of single academic disciplines. Readers interested in the Halstead formula are directed to the 1991 publication, *The Cost of Higher Education*, available from Research Associates of Washington at the address cited in Chapter 2.

The issue of productivity is no less problematic. If the researcher's sole interest is instructional productivity, there are common factors for assessing it – headcount enrollment, student credit hours taught, degrees granted, and so forth. But at most institutions, instruction comprises less than 100% of a faculty member's time. How is non-instructional productivity measured, particularly in units where external funding is not readily available. Administrative productivity is equally thorny. How should productivity in a registrar's office or an institutional research office be measured?

As complex as the issues surrounding cost and productivity analyses are, the need for reliable information cannot be ignored. Such data are essential both to effective institutional decision-making and to demonstrating economy and efficiency to external constituencies, some of whom are occasionally less than friendly. The remainder of this chapter will focus on how institutions can begin to look at cost and productivity despite problematic concerns.

Getting Started

1. <u>Instructional Productivity</u>. When looking at the issue of productivity, the researcher is trying to determine some measure of output per unit of personnel. Academic productivity is the logical starting point of a college or university institutional research office. The most common productivity measures in this setting include such ratios as "student credit hours taught per FTE faculty," "teaching credit hours per FTE faculty," or "FTE students taught per FTE faculty." As well, many institutions provide faculty with release time to pursue externally sponsored research and public service projects. An appropriate productivity measure for this type of activity would be "sponsored funds per FTE faculty." However, as the researcher prepares to develop data to capture these ratios, certain cautions should be exercised.

Ensuring precision and clarity in definitions is the first step. Each of the foregoing productivity measures has "FTE faculty" as the divisor. However, the term "faculty" may not mean the same thing in each instance. If the focus of analysis is <u>instructional</u> activity, then "faculty" should reflect all individuals who teach. This would include tenure and tenure-track faculty, as well as part-time, adjunct instructors, graduate assistants, and professionals with teaching responsibilities. On the other hand, several major universities employ research faculty who do no teaching at all; these individuals would be excluded from an instructional workload faculty divisor.

The proportion of time spent in teaching requires similar precision and definition. An aggregate ratio such as "student credit hours taught per FTE faculty" is instructive, but will surely lead to requests for additional information. What proportion of those credit hours are being taught by regular faculty on appointment? How many credit hours in introductory level courses are being taught by tenured faculty members? What proportion of an individual faculty member's teaching is done as part of the contractually administered load, and what proportion is done for supplemental pay?

In preparing to analyze instructional productivity, it is important to aggregate data from individual faculty to department/program level, then to school/college level, and if applicable, finally to university/institutional level. Table 6.1 which is an actual production report at the authors' institution, illustrates how this might be achieved. Individual faculty in a given department – in this instance, History – are displayed along with course-by-course listings of their respective teaching loads for a given semester. Courses that are dual listed (offered at both the undergraduate and graduate levels) and cross listed (offered under two or more departments' call letters) are clearly indicated to avoid double counting the number of courses taught.

Information about the course, including course type (regularly scheduled or supervised independent study), course credit value, teaching credit hours, students enrolled, and student credit hours (course credit value multiplied by number of students enrolled) are also shown. Similarly, descriptive information about the faculty member is also presented, including academic rank, tenure status, department to which the faculty member's salary is budgeted, and whether or not supplemental payment for teaching is received.

Figure 3, which shows only three faculty members, is an abbreviated version of the actual report. The actual report would include everyone teaching History courses during a given semester, including part-time personnel who would clearly be identified as such with an appropriate title under the "academic rank" heading. The departmental summary at the bottom of the figure shows total students enrolled in History courses, total teaching credits, and student credit hours. The data are presented for regularly scheduled courses, for supervised independent study, and an overall total. The data are also arrayed by lower division (courses with 100-200 sequence numbers), upper division (courses with 300-400 sequence numbers), and graduate course level (courses with 500-900 sequence numbers).

The summary is simply the total aggregation of the data displayed for each of the individual faculty members. The departmental summaries can be further aggregated to larger relevant organizational units. By keying on the individual data elements identified in the foregoing example, it is possible to generate answers to the question, "Who is teaching what and to whom." And it is relatively easy to generate productivity ratios such as "student credit hours or teaching credit hours per FTE faculty."

When looking at instructional productivity in academic units, it is useful to take a two-pronged approach. An "origin of course" analysis would examine the workload of all faculty teaching courses budgeted to a given department, regardless of whether the instructor's salary is budgeted to that department. Figure 3 is an example of such an analysis. All of the courses in the example have the "HIST" course prefix, indicating that they are budgeted to the History Department. This includes HIST467/652, a dual-listed course taught by Assistant Professor Brown, whose salary is actually paid by the Political Science Department.

Part 1

Figure 3:

College of Arts and Science: History

Name	Rank/Course	Section(s)	Tenure/Credits	Home Dept/Course Type	Students Enrolled	Teaching Credits	Student Credits	S=Supplemental Pay
Smith	**CHAIRPERSON**		Yes	**History**				S=None
	HIST268	1	3hrs.	Regular Schedule	15.0	3.0	45.0	
	TOTAL				15.0	3.0	45.0	
Jones	**PROFESSOR**		Yes	**History**				S=None
	HIST205	1	3hrs.	Regular Schedule	100.0	3.0	300.0	
	HIST307	2	3hrs.	Regular Schedule	37.0	3.0	111.0	
	HIST666	1	1-6hrs.	Supervised Study	1.0	1.0	3.0	
	TOTAL			▶	138.0	7.0	414.0	
Brown	**ASST. PROFESSOR**		Yes	**Political Science**				S=None
	HIST467	1	3hrs.	Regular Schedule	8.0	3.0	24.0	
	400-LEVEL SECTION MEETS WITH A 600-LEVEL							
	HIST652	1	3hrs.	Regular Schedule	3.0		9.0	
	CROSS LIST: POSC629							
	600-LEVEL SECTION MEETS WITH A 400-LEVEL							
	TOTAL				11.0	3.0	33.0	

86

Part 2

Figure 3:

College of Arts and Science: History

DEPARTMENTAL SUMMARY

		Students Enrolled	Teaching Credits	Student Credits
REGULARLY SCHEDULED COURSES	LOWER DIVISION (000-299)	2205.0	102.0	6615.0
	UPPER DIVISION (300-499)	919.0	75.0	2757.0
	GRADUATE (500-999)	130.0	33.0	390.0
	DEPARTMENT TOTAL	3254.0	210.0	9762.0
SUPERVISED STUDY COURSES	LOWER DIVISION (000-299)	0.0	0.0	0.0
	UPPER DIVISION (300-499)	7.0	7.0	24.0
	GRADUATE (500-999)	33.0	33.0	147.0
	DEPARTMENT TOTAL	40.0	40.0	171.0
REGULARLY SCHEDULED AND SUPERVISED COURSES	LOWER DIVISION (000-299)	2205.0	102.0	6615.0
	UPPER DIVISION (300-499)	926.0	82.0	2781.0
	GRADUATE (500-999)	163.0	68.0	537.0
	DEPARTMENT TOTAL	3294.0	250.0	9933.0

The alternative analytical approach would be "origin of instructor" wherein workload is tallied and summarized based upon the department to which the faculty member's salary is budgeted. In that instance, Assistant Professor Brown and the History courses he teaches would disappear from the History Department and would appear under the Political Science Department listing. If Professor Jones were teaching a course in the Department of Urban Affairs, say URAF 650, that course would appear next to her name along with the History courses she is teaching, in an "origin of instructor" analysis. In the current environment of scarce economic resources, it is important to encourage interdisciplinary activity and interdepartmental cooperation. "Origin of instructor" analysis accommodates those department chairs who want to ensure that they receive credit for workload done by faculty on "loan" to another department or program.

2. Research and Service Productivity. If the focus is research and service productivity, as measured by sponsored funds per FTE faculty, then the occasional teaching personnel that were included in the previous example would be excluded in this instance. The focal group would be tenure and tenure-track personnel who have research and service expectations as part of their administered workload. The research faculty whose sole responsibility is sponsored research activity would also be included in this divisor. Full-time equivalency calculations are generally performed at the institutional level. In instances where part-time teaching personnel are assigned an "FTEness," many institutions assume a normative administered teaching load of 12 course credit hours per semester for a typical faculty member, and divide by 12 the teaching credit hours assigned to each part time faculty member to arrive at full time equivalency.

3. Cost Analysis. In approaching the financial side of the cost and productivity issue, it is important that institutional research offices develop close working relationships with the budget and accounting offices at the college or university. Most institutions utilize conventional cost accounting practices where budget and expenditure transactions are assigned "object codes" and "function codes" Object codes describe upon what funds are being spent: salaries and benefits, support accounts such as travel, supplies, and equipment. Function codes describe the functional purpose of the expenditure, i.e., instruction, academic support, student support, sponsored research, sponsored service, institutional support, and so on.

By working closely with the financial office(s) at the college, the institutional researcher can develop a matrix similar to that in Table 6.1, which shows, for any given department or program, expenditures by object and function. Every college and university reports expenditure data, by function, in the annual institutional financial report and on the IPEDS Survey of Institutional Finances. Since the data can be aggregated upward to the full institutional level, they can be disaggregated downward to individual, organizational budget units. Developing production reports to achieve this goal may require substantial collaborative time and energy between institutional researchers and financial offices, but it is well worth the time invested. The ability to provide departmental chairs and unit directors with financial detail such as that in Table 6.1, derived directly from the institutional accounting system, enhances the perceived integrity and impact of cost or productivity measures.

Using data from a departmental summary such as that in Table 6.1, it is possible to take total expenditures under the "instruction" column and divide by the total student credit hours taught by that department to arrive at "direct instructional cost per student credit hour." Or the researcher can combine total expenditures for sponsored research and sponsored public service and divide by the appropriate aggregation of full time equivalent faculty to arrive at "direct sponsored activity per FTE faculty." **Direct** expenditures are emphasized because it is probably best for the institutional research office to deal in those instructional costs which can be directly tied to the accounting system and which have the most general comparability. In looking at full cost analysis, it is difficult to find two institutions that calculate full cost in exactly the same fashion, and this pattern filters down to the departmental level. The reader will recall the Halstead formula for full cost described earlier in the chapter. As a broad institutional gauge, it is useful; as a fiscal tool at the departmental or programmatic level, it lacks precision.

4. Interinstitutional Comparisons. The analytical approaches to developing instructional cost and productivity measures described in the chapter are useful for making interdepartmental comparisons within a given college or university. However, comparative data become even more useful when one can compare the direct cost of a student credit hour in History at Institution X with that at Institution Y. Little has been done with respect to interinstitutional cost and productivity comparisons at the academic department and/or program level, largely because of methodological difficulties inherent in such comparisons. The University of Delaware undertook a major national study of comparative productivity and cost measures at the academic program level in 1993-94, and copies of the study results and discussion of the methodology employed may be obtained by writing to the principal investigator:

Michael F. Middaugh
Director of Institutional Research and Planning
University of Delaware
Newark, DE 19716

5. Administrative Productivity. The discussion in this chapter thus far has been academic costs and productivity. The academic units have a fairly standard set of measures against which to measure productivity, e.g. students taught, student credit hours, and teaching credit hours. No comparable commonly defined and widely accepted measures exist for administrative functions. Nonetheless, it is important that institutions be as concerned about productivity, efficiency, and cost effectiveness among administrative units as they are among academic departments.

Some useful writing with respect to administrative productivity already exists. The New Directions for Institutional Research volume, *Containing Costs and Improving Productivity in Higher Education*, previously cited, contains a number of chapters on the subject. Additionally, William E. Massy delivered a paper at the October 1989 Forum for College Financing in Annapolis, Maryland titled, "Productivity improvement strategies for college and university administration and support services." Dr. Massy is Director of the Stanford Institute for Higher Education Research at Stanford University, and interested readers can contact him at that institution. The National Association of College and University Business Officers (NACUBO) has also undertaken a national benchmarking project to provide comparative data with respect to cost and productivity in major administrative areas.

Researchers interested in learning more about this benchmarking project might wish to read the December 1993 issue of *NACUBO Business Officer*, *27* (6), 21-31, or contact NACUBO directly at One Dupont Circle, Washington DC 20036.

Assessing instructional cost and productivity is a new horizon for institutional research, and is one that will increasingly determine the vitality and relevance of institutional research at individual colleges and universities. This chapter introduces the researcher to some of the issues in this area and provides the appropriate resources to initiate a serious cost and productivity analysis at any institution, regardless of size or type.

CHAPTER SEVEN:
SOME IMPLEMENTATION STRATEGIES

The first six chapters of this book have introduced the literature, resources, and strategies that underpin a broad range of activity within the scope of "institutional research." How can this information be translated into practice? No institutional research office does everything that has been discussed thus far. The key to developing and maintaining a viable research program is to make certain that the analytical activities of the office are relevant to the information needs of the campus president and other senior leaders. That can be achieved only by listening carefully and thoroughly understanding the campus culture. Cultivating a network of deans, department chairs, and senior administrative directors on campus certainly accelerates the learning curve.

In considering how to implement an effective program of institutional research, there are certain guidelines that are helpful. Taken from the authors' own professional experiences, and those of colleagues who have shared their experiences with us at regional and national institutional research association meetings, we offer what we term several basic guidelines of institutional research.

First Guideline: Firmly establish the centrality of your Office of Institutional Research in coordinating campus databases and disseminating institutional data. While "ownership" or "stewardship" of databases should reside in the offices primarily responsible for data collection and entry (e.g., student records in the Registrar's Office, financial data in the Budget Office, etc.), Institutional Research should be the central actor in the coordinating process.

Coordination refers to such activities as determining when to freeze official campus data bases (i.e., extract from the live computer files those fixed data sets that will be used for all internal, external, and historical reporting in all areas of operations), as well as reviewing and checking data integrity through routine reporting processes. It is particularly helpful if Institutional Research is designated by the president as the "official" clearinghouse for all data used in internal and external reports developed by units across the campus.

Second Guideline: Establish a friendly, professional relationship with the director of computing center and his/her programming staff. Depending on programming skills of the personnel in the institutional research office, it may be necessary to communicate with computing center personnel about programming new production reports, making modifications in existing reports, submitting requests for series of enrollment or financial aid reports, or adding data elements to existing data files. It is also often necessary to obtain consulting advice about computing software, hardware, pricing, telecommunications, and so on. A strong working relationship between the institutional research and computing center can ease the professional burden of both staffs.

Third Guideline: Whenever possible, obtain data from primary sources. Using existing data elements within established data bases strengthens your research. Most likely, the Registrar's Office has already collected basic demographic information from students at the time of initial registration (age, gender, ethnicity, permanent residence, current and cumulative grade point average, etc.), and may ask for verification of the same data during subsequent registrations. These are reliable data already residing in the student record system. The same is true for admissions data (e.g., high school grades, standardized test scores, sending high school, etc.), personnel data (e.g., faculty rank, tenure status, highest earned degree, etc.) and other standard data elements cutting across all campus functions.

This guideline holds particular importance with respect to survey data. It may be possible to shorten surveys not collecting information that already exists in the institution's computer files. Of course, this means that survey respondents must provide a social security number or other institutional identifier in order for the researcher to identify respondents. If surveys are administered anonymously, the researcher usually has no choice but to request all necessary information on the questionnaire. These comments lead to two corollaries to the Third Guideline:

Fourth Guideline: Many times, institutional researchers find themselves conducting surveys to answer almost every question that comes up. This may lead to situations where undergraduate students or other populations become oversampled. Consequently, another useful guideline is to minimize the use of surveys where possible: Use surveys or focus interviews to collect data *if no other* access exists.

If surveys are to be utilized, the researcher has two options: 1) Use a commercially prepared, professionally published instrument from a vendor, or 2) develop a locally-prepared instrument. Student satisfaction, attrition, alumni, and other student surveys all focus on essentially the same issue from year to year and from campus to campus. Vendors understand this and have developed standardized survey forms to address generic issues, and in most instances, provide the opportunity for campuses to ask several institution specific questions on the commercially prepared survey form.

A major advantage to commercial surveys is that national normative data are usually available so that an individual institution can be compared to others. As well, the vendor has addressed such technical problems as instrument reliability and validity. If the survey results bring bad news to the campus community, it is helpful to compare a single institution's results to other schools. It may often be the case that the bad news is similar at comparable schools or that what appears to be bad at a single school is actually better than a normative sample of competitors.

Also, if an analysis cannot be attacked on anything else, the technical construction of the survey becomes an issue. A commercially prepared instrument removes that vulnerability. Locally-prepared instruments offer none of these advantages, and require significant investments of time and energy to properly construct.

If it is decided to use a locally designed and prepared instrument, keep the questionnaire brief. A basic tenet of survey research is that the return rate is inversely proportional to the length of the survey. Ask only the information that is needed to answer questions which generated the survey. While a one to two page survey is best, a four-page survey that is well-designed is acceptable. Beyond that, many individuals are reluctant to invest the time to answer a more lengthy questionnaire.

Ideally, the Office of Institutional Research coordinates survey administration on campus. The operative word here is "ideally." Ad hoc surveys proliferate across many higher education campuses. The notion that any data need can be solved with a survey is pervasive. Consequently, members of the campus community, particularly students, may be surveyed time and time again. If the same students are repeatedly asked to fill out various surveys, response rates will suffer. To the extent that the institutional researcher can eliminate multiple surveys to the same individual through coordination of survey administrations, return rates will prosper.

Fifth Guideline: Write reports that are easy to understand. Most reports and analyses are targeted at senior campus administrators. These are busy individuals who, for the most part, may have forgotten such concepts as levels of significance, degrees of freedom, and null hypotheses, but are interested in the study's findings and their implications for the campus.

It is also worthwhile to remember that descriptive statistics (averages, frequencies, cross-tabulations, percentages) are easier for the lay person to understand than advanced statistics (factor analysis, multiple regression, discriminant analysis). Reports to senior executives need not contain a full description of statistical treatment so long as the researcher has the details of the study available if needed. The report can simply say that, "Adding weights to high school honors courses contributes little beyond high school grades alone when making predictions of students' first year grades," without going into a detailed discussion of stepwise multiple regression. Make certain, however, that the regression equations to back up the statement are at hand, if requested.

Sixth Guideline: Keep reports brief and concise. Remember that a two page Executive Summary is more likely to be read than is a 25 page report. If written well, the Executive Summary may pique the reader's interest and invite him/her to delve into the full report. A parallel guideline is the time worn phrase, "A picture is worth a thousand words." Frequently, researchers may find that a chart or graph can replace much unnecessary text. Writing with brevity and clarity are the keys to having your reports read and acted upon by senior officials.

We encourage institutional researchers to attend regional or national workshops which offer professional develop activities on effective report writing and data presentation. A tremendous amount of labor is usually involved in many institutional research efforts: methodological steps are considered and agreed upon, samples are drawn, surveys are administered, data are keyed into computer files and verified, and statistical analyses are run. It is a potential shame to negate much of the preliminary work by producing a final report that is badly written.

Seventh Guideline. If institutional research is to remain a viable and important force in policy analysis and decision support at an individual college, it should never be complacent. The researcher should try to be visionary, constantly seeking new ways to generate factual information that leads to concrete policy activity. The institutional researcher can use a variety of tools – for example, computer networks and professional meetings – to continually scan the environment. What important policy changes may the federal government be initiating that will affect the institution? Is the population of high school seniors growing or shrinking in areas important to the college or university? What is the state legislature thinking about outcomes assessment?

Chapter 2 described a number of professional associations, journals, and other sources for on-going dialogue with colleagues as to the state of the art. We encourage institutional researchers to use these resources. Read, write, attend meetings, present papers, and publish. Find out what other institutional researchers are thinking and doing, and how they're doing it. Constantly test the currency and validity of the research methodology in use. It is all too easy to become comfortable with a given methodological approach to a problem. That is not to suggest that the wheel needs to be re-invented each time a particular issue arises; however, it is wise to constantly check to make certain that the wheel is still round and turning, and getting the institution the information it needs.

Appendix 1
Sample AIR Internet Newsletter

Date: Tue, 29 Mar 1994 12:08:29 -0700
Reply-To: NELSON_L@SALT.PLU.EDU
Sender: Institutional Researchers/University Planners <AIR-L%VTVM1.BITNET@UDELVM.UDEL.EDU>
From: "LARRY NELSON, PLU INSTITUTIONAL RESEARCH" <NELSON_L@SALT.PLU.EDU>
Subject: The Electronic AIR, 3/29/94, Part C
To: Multiple recipients of list AIR-L <AIR-L%VTVM1.BITNET@UDELVM.UDEL.EDU>

```
* * * * * * * * * * * * The Electronic  AIR * * * * * * * * * * * * *
*                                                                   *
*              The Electronic Newsletter                            *
*       of the Association for Institutional Research (AIR)         *
*           Serving Institutional Research Professionals            *
*    and those Engaged in Mgt. Research, Policy Analysis & Planning *
*                                                                   *
*      March 29, 1994. . . . . . . . . . .Volume 14, Number 6       *
*                          Part C                                   *
*        Editor - Larry Nelson, Pacific Lutheran University         *
*                  <NELSON_L@SALT.PLU.EDU>                          *
* * * * * * * * * * * * * * * * * * * * * * * * * * * * * * * * * * *
*                  Current Subscribers = 1161                       *
* * * * * * * * * * * * * * * * * * * * * * * * * * * * * * * * * * *


* * * * * * * * * * * * * * TABLE OF CONTENTS * * * * * * * * * * * *
* NEWS - AERA/Spencer Doctoral Research Training Fellowship Programs *
* HELP - Administrative Evaluations                                 *
* HELP - Employee Suggestion Programs as a Source of Cost Saving Ideas*
* HELP - Automating Factbooks                                       *
* POSITION LISTING - University of Dayton (OH)                      *
* POSITION LISTING - Nat'l. Institute of Independent Colleges & Univ. *
* POSITION LISTING - University of California, Santa Cruz (CA)      *
* POSITION LISTING - Azusa Pacific University (CA)                  *
* PARTING THOUGHT                                                   *
* * * * * * * * * * * * * * * * * * * * * * * * * * * * * * * * * * *


* * * * * * * * * * * * * * * * * * * * * * * * * * * * * * * * * * *
* NEWS - AERA/Spencer Doctoral Research Training Fellowship Programs *
* Reprinted From: American Educational Research Association List     *
*                 <AERA@ASUACAD.BITNET>                             *
* * * * * * * * * * * * * * * * * * * * * * * * * * * * * * * * * * *
```

The American Educational Research Association, in partnership with
the Spencer Foundation, announce a program to increase the cadre of new,
well-prepared educational researchers. Funds are available to provide
fellowship support for promising graduate students in educational
research, and to provide a program of educational experiences designed
to help new researchers become contributing members of the community.

The fellowship program is targeted for full time graduate students
approximately midway through their doctoral programs, generally in their
second year of a full-time program. Fellows will be provided with
unique access to the community of educational researchers and with a
mentoring and cohort network that would probably be unavailable to them
at their institutions.

Applications are sought for two fellowship programs; each will make
awards for the start of the 1994-1995 academic year.

(1) The AERA/SPENCER 1 year Fellowship Program will make awards
averaging $16,000 plus travel funds for professional development
activities. Fellows will have, in addition to financial support,
opportunities to participate in a number of activities designed to
complement and extend the education and training they receive at their

home institutions. Such experiences will be designed to facilitate the
entry and socialization of new researchers into the field. Activities
include a national mentor component, two 1 week summer institutes with a
distinguished national faculty, unique participation experiences at the
AERA Annual Meeting, experiences at the professional meetings of other
disciplines and access to an electronic network linking fellows,
mentors, and AERA staff. Spencer Foundation funds will support up to 12
Fellowships for the 1994-1995 academic year.

(2) The AERA/SPENCER Travel Fellowships of $3,000 are designed for
students who receive financial support at their home institution, but
wish to take part in the professional enhancement activities of the
fellowship program enumerated above. The 1 year Travel Fellowships do
not provide for a national mentor or monthly stipends. Spencer
Foundations funds will support as many as 10 travel fellowships for
1994-1995.

Deadline for receipt of applications is May 20, 1994. Applicants
will be notified by the end of June, 1994. Minorities and persons with
disabilities are encouraged to apply. Application forms for the two
programs are available by contacting:
          AERA
          1230 17th Street
          Washington DC, 20036
          Phone (202) 223-9485 FAX (202) 775-1824

* *
* HELP - Administrative Evaluations   *
* David Frace, Essex Community College <DEF0@ECC.CC.VT.EDU>   *
* *

At Essex Community College, we are in the process of developing
administrative evaluations. Each major administrative dean has to
evaluate 33% of his administrative units each year. Since we have not
had this request in the past, it is new territory for us. To help us
format such a program, I would like to look at how others have
accomplished this feat at other campuses.

Please forward to me any sample administrative evaluations that your
campus may have completed over the past. Thank you very much for your
assistance as we can use all the help we can get.
          David E. Frace
          Essex Community College
          7201 Rossville Boulevard
          Baltimore, Md 21237
          Phone: (410) 780-6401 FAX: (410) 574-2172
          E-Mail: <DEF0@ECC.bitnet>

* *
* HELP - Employee Suggestion Programs as a Source of Cost Saving Ideas*
* Kay Palmer, Oakland Comm. Coll.<KEPALMER%OCC.bitnet@CUNYVM.CUNY.EDU>*
* *

We currently have a committee at Oakland Community College looking
at the possibility of introducing an employee suggestion program
designed to find cost saving measures. It has been suggested that the
scheme would include a reward system for employees who devise real cost
saving measures. We know of many examples in industry of this type of
program but have no knowledge of anyone in the higher education sphere
who is operating such a scheme. Could anyone enlighten us and provide
details of existing programs? Please contact:
          Kay Palmer

Department of Institutional Planning & Analysis
Oakland Community College
27055 Orchard Lake Road
Farmington Hills, MI 48334-4579
Phone: (810)471-7746   FAX: (810) 471-7544

* *
* HELP - Automating Factbooks   *
* Joe Meyer, Southwest Texas State University <JM01@academia.swt.edu> *
* *

I would like to get opinions on the feasibility and sensibility of
automating college or university "fact books". I have had several
ideas, all of which are rather complex, and I don't want to spend a lot
of time doing something that is more trouble that it is worth. I'll be
happy to summarize the results of this survey, but first, here are a few
of the ideas I've considered:

1.) Aggregate data to be included in the fact book into categories
    of ethnicity, sex, major, etc. and export the aggregated file
    as comma-delimited or other machine-readable data for import to
    a spreadsheet program or word processor.

2.) Use active links between a spreadsheet and a word processing
    software to automatically put the information in a spreadsheet
    into a word processing document.

3.) Use a series of linked spreadsheets and formulae to aggregate
    the data in some tables of the fact book into the results for
    other tables in the fact book. For instance, a table showing
    majors by school and department could be aggregated by formulae
    to produce a table of enrollment by department or enrollment by
    school.

The problem with all of these options is that movement of majors
from one department to another, renaming of majors, and other
formatting changes occur frequently and mean that portions of the fact
book must be re-arranged or reformatted each year.   This can be done
with a little caution in relatively simple spreadsheets, but when
things get too complicated, formulae can really get messed up quickly
when you try to move things in ways they should not be moved. Another
problem is the time taken by computers to execute these various steps.
Does anybody have what they consider to be the ultimate balance between
automation and simplicity in producing a yearly fact book?
        Joe Meyer, Assistant Director
        Institutional Research & Planning
        Southwest Texas State University
        E-Mail: <JM01@ADMIN.SWT.EDU>

* *
* POSITION LISTING - University of Dayton (OH)   *
* Carolyn Benz, University of Dayton <BENZ@DAYTON.BITNET>   *
* *

The Department of Educational Administration at the University of
Dayton announces a search for an Asst./Assoc. Professor to teach
educational research and statistics beginning in August, 1994.

Prefer doctorate in educational administration, experience as a
school administrator, college teaching experience, and experience
working with Ph.D. students on dissertation committees. The application
deadline is April 15.

Letters of application with vita, names, addresses and telephone
numbers of three references should be sent to:
        Dr. William R. Drury
        Search Committee
        Department of Educational Administration
        The University of Dayton
        Dayton, OH 45469-0534

* *
* POSITION LISTING - Nat'l. Institute of Independent Colleges & Univ. *
* Reprinted From: American Educational Research Association List   *
* *

        The position of Policy Analyst is currently open at the National
Institute of Independent Colleges and Universities (NIICU). NIICU is
the research arm of the National Association of Independent Colleges and
Universities (NAICU) which represents private colleges and universities
on public policy issues with the legislative, executive, and judicial
branches of the federal government.

        The Policy Analyst reports to the Executive Director of NIICU and
works as part of a team in conducting research and analyses of the
impact of public policies on the nation's independent colleges and
universities. Candidates for this position should have strong
quantitative and computer skills, be familiar with public policies
affecting private colleges and universities, have strong writing and
communications skills, be able to represent NIICU to its membership and .
external constituencies, and be able to work closely with other staff
members. A graduate degree in a relevant discipline is preferred. The
salary is competitive and fringe benefits are excellent.

        Preferential consideration will be given to applications received by
April 22, 1994. NIICU is an equal opportunity, affirmative action
employer.

        Interested candidates should send a letter of application, resume
and the names, addresses, and telephone numbers of at least four
references to:
        Director of Personnel
        NIICU
        122 C Street, N.W., Suite 750,
        Washington, D.C. 20001-2190.

* *
* POSITION LISTING - University of California, Santa Cruz (CA)   *
* Randy Nelson, UC - Santa Cruz <randy@cats.ucsc.edu>   *
* *

                        Senior Administrative Analyst

        Reports to the Director of Institutional Research and Policy
Studies. Primary areas of responsibility include:

Data administration:
        Provides oversight for the definition of data elements across all
campus database systems. Identifies and resolves differences in data
element definitions across systems. Ensures that data elements are
consistent with users' needs.

Chairs the Data Warehouse Committee:
        Oversee a client-server database containing information on the

100

Appendix 2
Standard Production Reports

UNIVERSITY OF DELAWARE
STUDENT INFORMATION SYSTEM REPORT
UNDERGRADUATE STUDENTS

SEMESTER: Fall 1993

93F END OF TERM

COLLEGE, SEX, CLASS, AND RESIDENT STATUS

	COMB. TOTAL	FRESHMAN		SOPHOMORE		JUNIOR		SENIOR		NON-DEGREE		TOTAL	
		N	R	N	R	N	R	N	R	N	R	N	R
COLLEGE OF AGRICULTURAL SCIENCES													
MALES FULL-TIME	273	35	34	42	35	27	39	21	40	0	0	125	148
PART-TIME	76	6	4	0	8	2	19	4	33	0	0	12	64
****	349	41	38	42	43	29	58	25	73	0	0	137	212
FEMALES FULL-TIME	243	43	27	41	30	20	29	21	30	0	2	125	118
PART-TIME	36	3	4	3	4	3	8	3	8	0	0	12	24
****	279	46	31	44	34	23	37	24	38	0	2	137	142
TOTAL	628	87	69	86	77	52	95	49	111	0	2	274	354
COLLEGE OF ARTS AND SCIENCE													
MALES FULL-TIME	3338	610	435	525	417	474	347	260	262	6	2	1875	1463
PART-TIME	450	18	55	31	89	21	61	34	139	0	2	104	346
****	3788	628	490	556	506	495	408	294	401	6	4	1979	1809
FEMALES FULL-TIME	4205	943	441	736	440	615	332	414	273	11	0	2719	1486
PART-TIME	496	22	65	25	80	22	94	32	152	2	2	103	393
****	4701	965	506	761	520	637	426	446	425	13	2	2822	1879
TOTAL	8489	1593	996	1317	1026	1132	834	740	826	19	6	4801	3688
COLLEGE OF BUSINESS AND ECONOMICS													
MALES FULL-TIME	965	172	58	180	69	164	76	147	95	4	0	667	298
PART-TIME	88	4	3	3	8	4	15	20	31	0	0	31	57
****	1053	176	61	183	77	168	91	167	126	4	0	698	355
FEMALES FULL-TIME	708	132	43	141	46	130	50	102	63	0	1	505	203
PART-TIME	68	0	2	3	6	3	14	9	31	0	0	15	53
****	776	132	45	144	52	133	64	111	94	0	1	520	256
TOTAL	1829	308	106	327	129	301	155	278	220	4	1	1218	611
COLLEGE OF EDUCATION													
MALES FULL-TIME	37	4	13	1	4	2	0	1	12	0	0	8	29
PART-TIME	8	1	2	1	0	0	1	0	3	0	0	2	6
****	45	5	15	2	4	2	1	1	15	0	0	10	35
FEMALES FULL-TIME	710	82	83	129	76	105	58	101	73	3	0	420	290
PART-TIME	65	0	2	1	5	4	9	20	20	1	3	26	39
****	775	82	85	130	81	109	67	121	93	4	3	446	329
TOTAL	820	87	100	132	85	111	68	122	108	4	3	456	364
COLLEGE OF ENGINEERING													
MALES FULL-TIME	662	126	84	101	49	75	61	78	88	0	0	380	282
PART-TIME	53	2	6	4	9	2	6	7	17	0	0	15	38
****	715	128	90	105	58	77	67	85	105	0	0	395	320
FEMALES FULL-TIME	193	35	26	34	15	14	16	33	20	0	0	116	77
PART-TIME	9	1	3	1	1	0	1	1	1	0	0	3	6
****	202	36	29	35	16	14	17	34	21	0	0	119	83
TOTAL	917	164	119	140	74	91	84	119	126	0	0	514	403

OFFICE OF THE REGISTRAR
INSTITUTIONAL RESEARCH
REPORT ID: RPT426

UNIVERSITY OF DELAWARE
STUDENT INFORMATION SYSTEM REPORT
UNDERGRADUATE STUDENTS

SIPR426   PAGE: 0001
01/17/94   17:19

93F END OF TERM

SEMESTER: Fall 1993

COLLEGE, MAJOR, CLASS AND SEX

COLLEGE OF AGRICULTURAL SCIENCES

Code	Major	COMB. TOTAL	FR M	FR F	SO M	SO F	JR M	JR F	SR M	SR F	ND M	ND F	TOTAL M	TOTAL F
ABM	Agricultural Business Management	61	16	4	7	4	12	4	11	3	0	0	46	15
AEC	Agricultural Economics	10	0	2	3	0	2	1	1	1	0	0	6	4
AED	Agricultural Education	5	0	1	2	0	1	0	0	1	0	0	3	2
AET	Agricultural Engineering Technolog	48	10	2	2	0	10	3	19	2	0	0	41	7
ANS	Animal Science	222	22	48	21	49	9	29	11	32	0	1	63	159
ENT	Entomology	72	7	8	16	12	9	4	10	6	0	0	42	30
EPP	Entomology and Plant Pathology	3	1	1	0	2	0	2	1	0	0	0	2	1
ESOS	Environmental Soil Sciences	14	3	2	2	2	0	1	3	1	0	0	8	6
ETM	Engineering Technology	70	3	0	3	2	30	1	28	3	0	0	64	6
FSC	Food Science	26	1	4	3	2	0	6	8	2	0	0	12	14
GAG	General Agriculture	21	6	2	3	0	3	0	5	2	0	0	17	4
PLS	Plant Science	1	0	0	0	0	0	0	0	1	0	0	0	1
PLSS	Plant and Soil Sciences	75	10	3	10	7	13	8	11	11	1	1	45	30
	TOTALS	628	79	77	85	78	87	60	96	62	0	2	349	279

COLLEGE OF ARTS AND SCIENCE

Code	Major	COMB. TOTAL	FR M	FR F	SO M	SO F	JR M	JR F	SR M	SR F	ND M	ND F	TOTAL M	TOTAL F
AMI	Applied Music - Instrumental	10	1	1	1	0	1	0	5	1	0	0	8	2
AMP	Applied Music - Piano	3	0	0	0	1	0	0	2	0	0	0	2	1
AMS	American Studies	12	0	0	2	2	2	3	2	1	0	0	6	6
AMV	Applied Music - Voice	12	3	0	2	0	2	0	2	3	0	0	9	3
ANT	Anthropology	47	5	8	8	6	2	7	4	6	0	1	19	28
ARC	Art Conservation	24	0	8	3	4	0	6	0	3	0	0	3	21
ARH	Art History	60	1	8	5	10	4	12	2	18	0	0	12	48
ART	Art	269	27	51	30	57	27	40	14	21	1	1	99	170
ASU	Arts and Sciences - Undeclared	2088	522	616	364	328	113	82	40	19	2	2	1041	1047
BIOC	Biochemistry	105	27	17	8	18	10	11	7	7	0	0	52	53
BIOL	Biological Sciences	822	75	150	112	132	91	105	60	96	0	1	338	484
CHEM	Chemistry	182	33	25	24	14	28	11	29	17	1	0	115	67
CIS	Computer and Information Sciences	206	39	31	46	10	41	10	38	15	0	0	164	42
CJ	Criminal Justice	462	48	41	53	41	105	62	78	42	1	0	286	176
CL	Comparative Literature	3	0	0	0	2	0	0	0	0	0	1	0	3
COM	Communication	132	0	0	2	7	19	41	13	50	0	0	34	98
COMI	Communication Interest	178	35	43	15	56	2	23	0	2	1	1	53	125
EC	Economics	31	6	1	4	4	6	0	8	2	0	0	24	7
ECA	Economics - Arts and Science	485	22	54	34	69	41	121	45	95	1	3	143	342
ENG	English	129	23	16	14	21	17	17	11	14	1	0	66	63
ENSC	Environmental Science	27	0	1	3	4	6	2	1	10	0	0	10	17
FA	Fine Arts	106	20	0	3	25	6	24	0	18	0	0	19	87
FLL	Foreign Languages and Literatures	1	0	0	0	0	0	0	0	1	0	0	0	1
FRPS	French/Political Science	68	3	0	11	1	15	11	12	13	0	2	41	27
GEOG	Geography	36	3	3	8	3	9	1	7	2	0	0	27	9
GEOL	Geology	3	2	2	1	0	0	0	0	1	0	0	2	1
GER	German	3	0	0	0	0	0	0	2	1	0	0	2	1
GPS	Geophysics	3	2	0	0	0	0	0	0	1	0	0	2	1
HFL	History and Foreign Languages	4	0	0	0	0	0	3	0	0	0	0	1	3

REPORT ID: UPS/820
INSTITUTIONAL RESEARCH
RUN TYPE: ACADEMIC YEAR
DATES: 07/01-06/30
YEARS: 84 85 86 87 88 89 90 91 92 93

UNIVERSITY OF DELAWARE
UNIVERSITY PLANNING SYSTEM
DEGREES AWARDED REPORT
Major Detail Report

College of Arts and Science
Social Sciences
Sociology

MAJOR / CONCENTRATION	YR	DEGREE BEG	DATES END	ASSOCIATE COUNT	PCT	BACHELOR COUNT	PCT	MASTERS COUNT	PCT	DOCTORATE COUNT	PCT	TOTAL COUNT	PCT
MAJOR: (CJ) Criminal Justice	84	07/01/83	06/30/84	0	0.0	128	100.0	0	0.0	0	0.0	128	100.0
	85	07/01/84	06/30/85	2	2.1	90	97.8	0	0.0	0	0.0	92	100.0
	86	07/01/85	06/30/86	2	1.9	100	98.0	0	0.0	0	0.0	102	100.0
	87	07/01/86	06/30/87	1	0.9	110	99.0	0	0.0	0	0.0	111	100.0
	88	07/01/87	06/30/88	1	0.8	115	99.1	0	0.0	0	0.0	116	100.0
	89	07/01/88	06/30/89	1	0.9	108	99.0	0	0.0	0	0.0	109	100.0
	90	07/01/89	06/30/90	1	0.7	139	99.2	0	0.0	0	0.0	140	100.0
	91	07/01/90	06/30/91	0	0.0	151	100.0	0	0.0	0	0.0	151	100.0
	92	07/01/91	06/30/92	0	0.0	172	100.0	0	0.0	0	0.0	172	100.0
	93	07/01/92	06/30/93	0	0.0	142	100.0	0	0.0	0	0.0	142	100.0
MAJOR: (CRM) Criminology	90	07/01/89	06/30/90	0	0.0	0	0.0	1	100.0	0	0.0	1	100.0
	92	07/01/91	06/30/92	0	0.0	0	0.0	1	100.0	0	0.0	1	100.0
	93	07/01/92	06/30/93	0	0.0	0	0.0	2	100.0	0	0.0	2	100.0
MAJOR: (SOC) Sociology	84	07/01/83	06/30/84	1	1.6	52	83.8	8	12.9	1	1.6	62	100.0
	85	07/01/84	06/30/85	0	0.0	44	91.6	3	6.2	1	2.0	48	100.0
	86	07/01/85	06/30/86	1	2.1	37	78.7	2	4.2	7	14.8	47	100.0
	87	07/01/86	06/30/87	1	1.9	43	84.3	3	5.8	4	7.8	51	100.0
	88	07/01/87	06/30/88	2	4.8	36	87.8	3	7.3	0	0.0	41	100.0
	89	07/01/88	06/30/89	0	0.0	30	83.3	2	5.5	4	11.1	36	100.0
	90	07/01/89	06/30/90	0	0.0	46	95.8	1	2.0	1	2.0	48	100.0
	91	07/01/90	06/30/91	0	0.0	44	86.2	5	9.8	2	3.9	51	100.0
	92	07/01/91	06/30/92	0	0.0	63	95.4	1	1.5	2	3.0	66	100.0
	93	07/01/92	06/30/93	0	0.0	52	86.6	4	6.6	4	6.6	60	100.0
MAJOR: (XSC) Sociology Education	84	07/01/83	06/30/84	0	0.0	1	100.0	0	0.0	0	0.0	1	100.0
	86	07/01/85	06/30/86	0	0.0	2	100.0	0	0.0	0	0.0	2	100.0
	87	07/01/86	06/30/87	0	0.0	1	100.0	0	0.0	0	0.0	1	100.0
	89	07/01/88	06/30/89	0	0.0	2	100.0	0	0.0	0	0.0	2	100.0
	90	07/01/89	06/30/90	0	0.0	1	100.0	0	0.0	0	0.0	1	100.0
	91	07/01/90	06/30/91	0	0.0	2	100.0	0	0.0	0	0.0	2	100.0
	93	07/01/92	06/30/93	0	0.0	1	100.0	0	0.0	0	0.0	1	100.0

Appendix 3
Weekly Admissions Report

HULLIHEN HALL
ADMISSIONS
FALL 1994

SIPM606   PAGE: 1
02/05/94   11:12
93-94 WEEKLY ADM REPORT

UNIVERSITY OF DELAWARE
STUDENT INFORMATION SYSTEM
WEEKLY ADMISSIONS CAMPUS SUMMARY REPORT

CAMPUS SUMMARY   NEW FRESHMEN APPLICANTS, THEIR SAT SCORES AND PGI BY ADMISSION STATUS, MAJOR AND RESIDENCY FOR THE
ENTERING CLASSES IN THE FALL OF 1992 AS OF 02/08/92. THE FALL OF 1993 AS OF 02/08/93
AND THE FALL OF 1994 AS OF 02/05/94 FOR THE
UNIVERSITY OF DELAWARE-NEWARK CAMPUS

	ALL APPLICANTS			ADMISSION DENIED			OFFERED ADMISSION			ACCEPTED ADMISSION (AC)			RATIO OF OFFERED TO ALL APPLICANTS			RATIO OF ACCEPTED TO OFFERED		
	92	93	94	92	93	94	92	93	94	92	93	94	92	93	94	92	93	94
COUNTS																		
RES	1269	1537	1510	31	59	73	859	1012	961	95	123	194	0.68	0.66	0.64	0.11	0.12	0.20
NON-RES	10012	10608	9373	1207	1482	1201	5992	5719	5397	166	169	208	0.60	0.54	0.58	0.03	0.03	0.04
TOTAL	11281	12145	10883	1238	1541	1274	6851	6731	6358	261	292	402	0.61	0.55	0.58	0.04	0.04	0.06
SAT VERBAL																		
RES	480	477	481	359	363	394	503	500	498	480	472	501	1.05	1.05	1.04	0.95	0.94	1.01
NON-RES	481	475	480	416	408	415	506	501	504	496	486	503	1.05	1.05	1.05	0.98	0.97	1.00
TOTAL	481	475	480	414	407	414	506	501	503	490	480	502	1.05	1.05	1.05	0.97	0.96	1.00
SAT MATH																		
RES	524	525	528	394	403	412	548	549	549	537	519	559	1.05	1.05	1.04	0.98	0.95	1.02
NON-RES	552	550	555	484	483	484	576	576	579	557	549	580	1.04	1.05	1.04	0.97	0.95	1.00
TOTAL	549	547	551	481	480	480	573	572	575	550	536	570	1.04	1.05	1.04	0.96	0.94	0.99
PGI																		
RES	2.35	2.38	2.41	0.97	1.10	1.34	2.61	2.64	2.63	2.57	2.51	2.65	1.11	1.11	1.09	0.98	0.95	1.01
NON-RES	2.45	2.44	2.46	1.64	1.71	1.68	2.73	2.75	2.72	2.71	2.73	2.76	1.11	1.13	1.11	0.99	0.99	1.01
TOTAL	2.44	2.44	2.45	1.63	1.69	1.66	2.72	2.73	2.70	2.66	2.64	2.70	1.11	1.12	1.10	0.98	0.97	1.00

***** END OF REPORT *****

HULLIHEN HALL
ADMISSIONS
FALL, 1994

SIPM607   PAGE: 2
02/05/94   11:12
93-94 WEEKLY ADM REPORT

UNIVERSITY OF DELAWARE
STUDENT INFORMATION SYSTEM
WEEKLY ADMISSIONS PROJECTED YIELD REPORT

NEW FRESHMEN - PROJECTED YIELD OF APPLICANTS AS OF 02/05/94
BY COLLEGE AND RESIDENT STATUS

COLLEGE	1994 ENROLLMENT TARGET	1993 ACTUAL YIELD	NUMBER NEEDED TO ADMIT	NUMBER OFFERED AS OF 02/05/94	NUMBER OF AC'S AS OF 02/05/94	PROJECTED YIELD
College of Agricultural Sciences						
RES	35	0.84	41	34	5	29
NON RESIDENT	85	0.33	257	122	6	41
TOTAL	120		298	156	11	70
College of Arts and Science						
RES	635	0.65	976	587	109	382
NON RESIDENT	1165	0.23	5065	3588	113	826
TOTAL	1800		6041	4175	222	1208
College of Business and Economics						
RES	160	0.66	242	86	19	57
NON RESIDENT	215	0.23	934	669	21	154
TOTAL	375		1176	755	40	211
College of Education						
RES	60	0.71	84	57	15	41
NON RESIDENT	90	0.27	333	228	18	62
TOTAL	150		417	285	33	103
College of Engineering						
RES	110	0.66	166	106	25	70
NON RESIDENT	145	0.22	659	419	28	93
TOTAL	255		825	525	53	163
College of Human Resources						
RES	40	0.80	50	23	6	19
NON RESIDENT	120	0.37	324	208	12	77
TOTAL	160		374	231	18	96
College of Nursing						
RES	20	0.74	27	37	10	28
NON RESIDENT	30	0.29	103	51	2	15
TOTAL	50		130	88	12	43
College of Physical Education						
RES	25	0.74	33	31	5	23
NON RESIDENT	65	0.35	185	112	8	40
TOTAL	90		218	143	13	63
University of Delaware - Newark Campus						
RES	1085	0.67	1619	961	194	644
NON RESIDENT	1915	0.24	7979	5397	208	1296
TOTAL	3000		9598	6358	402	1940

107

Appendix 4
Weekly Admissions Report With Quality Intervals

INSTITUTIONAL RESEARCH AND PLANNING

NEWARK CAMPUS
FALL 92,93 & 94 CURRENT
FIRST-TIME NEW STUDENTS

PAGE:
DATE: 05/10/94

FALL	TOTAL APPLICATIONS			TOTAL OFFERS			OFFERS AS % OF APPLICATIONS			TOTAL PAID DEPOSITS			PAID DEPOSITS AS % OF OFFERS		
	92	93	94	92	93	94	92	93	94	92	93	94	92	93	94
VERBAL SAT SCORES															
700-800	110	92	107	108	88	106	98.0	95.0	99.0	31	30	20	28.0	34.0	18.0
600-699	957	1003	846	918	981	821	95.0	97.0	97.0	230	248	120	25.0	25.0	14.0
500-599	4172	3989	3821	3704	3681	3541	88.0	92.0	92.0	1030	1000	640	27.0	27.0	18.0
400-499	6257	6362	5686	4356	4876	4496	69.0	76.0	76.0	1446	1665	982	33.0	33.0	21.0
300-399	1598	1950	1776	608	772	782	38.0	39.0	44.0	260	325	188	42.0	42.0	24.0
200-299	134	171	146	26	35	25	19.0	20.0	17.0	15	16	5	57.0	42.0	20.0
NO SCORE	126	159	120	31	50	19	24.0	31.0	15.0	20	26	2	64.0	52.0	10.0
AVERAGE	479	473	473	498	493	491				487	483	481			
MATH SAT SCORES															
700-800	608	704	631	580	672	611	95.0	95.0	96.0	128	144	88	22.0	21.0	14.0
600-699	3268	3313	3008	2884	3052	2788	88.0	92.0	92.0	711	763	392	24.0	25.0	14.0
500-599	5734	5752	5305	4404	4689	4372	76.0	81.0	82.0	1352	1469	888	30.0	31.0	20.0
400-499	3001	3082	3001	1657	1819	1816	55.0	59.0	60.0	725	775	521	43.0	42.0	28.0
300-399	573	653	588	191	193	181	33.0	29.0	30.0	93	109	64	48.0	56.0	35.0
200-299	44	63	49	4	8	3	9.0	12.0	6.0	3	6	2	75.0	75.0	66.0
NO SCORE	126	159	120	31	50	19	24.0	31.0	15.0	20	26	2	64.0	52.0	10.0
AVERAGE	546	544	544	565	564	563				546	545	540			
COMB SAT SCORES															
1500-1600	21	9	12	21	9	12	100.0	100.0	100.0	8	1	1	38.0	11.0	8.0
1400-1499	89	100	108	88	99	106	98.0	99.0	98.0	30	36	20	34.0	36.0	18.0
1300-1399	384	405	386	375	394	376	97.0	97.0	97.0	76	88	42	20.0	22.0	11.0
1200-1299	1089	1131	985	1037	1091	955	95.0	96.0	96.0	242	271	146	23.0	24.0	15.0
1100-1199	2409	2336	2171	2198	2208	2040	91.0	94.0	93.0	537	524	298	24.0	23.0	14.0
1000-1099	3755	3677	3339	3051	3241	2955	81.0	88.0	88.0	883	916	563	28.0	30.0	19.0
900-999	3199	3247	3057	2104	2424	2411	65.0	74.0	75.0	811	876	585	38.0	36.0	25.0
800-899	1554	1803	1728	676	778	833	43.0	43.0	48.0	334	367	236	49.0	47.0	28.0
700-799	540	614	599	150	166	153	27.0	27.0	25.0	81	102	53	54.0	61.0	34.0
600-699	143	191	155	18	23	27	12.0	12.0	17.0	8	5	10	44.0	65.0	37.0
BELOW-600	45	54	42	2	0	3	4.0	0.0	7.0	2	0	1	100.0	0.0	33.0
NO SCORE	126	159	120	31	50	19	24.0	31.0	15.0	20	26	2	64.0	52.0	10.0
AVERAGE	1025	1018	1017	1064	1057	1054				1034	1028	1021			
TOTALS	13354	13726	12702	9751	10483	9790	73.0	76.0	77.0	3032	3212	1957	31.0	31.0	19.0

NOTE: 1) AVERAGES DO NOT INCLUDE STUDENTS WITH NO SCORE

Appendix 5
Cohort Survival Analysis

TABLE 1: ENROLLMENT, DROPOUT RATES AND GRADUATION RATES
FOR FIRST-TIME FRESHMEN ON THE NEWARK CAMPUS (Total)

Entering Fall Term	Enrollment and Dropout Rates						Graduation Rates			
	1st Fall	2nd Fall	3rd Fall	4th Fall	5th Fall	6th Fall	within 3 yrs	within 4 yrs	within 5 yrs	Total
1983 N	2988	2498	2203	2105	636	114	10	1300	1907	2073
% enrollment	100.0%	83.6%	73.7%	70.4%	21.3%	3.8%	0.3%	43.5%	63.8%	69.4%
% dropout	0.0%	16.4%	26.3%	29.2%	35.2%	32.4%				
1984 N	3394	2839	2538	2437	695	123	9	1568	2219	2387
% enrollment	100.0%	83.6%	74.8%	71.8%	20.5%	3.6%	0.3%	46.2%	65.4%	70.3%
% dropout	0.0%	16.4%	25.2%	27.9%	33.3%	31.0%				
1985 N	3121	2632	2382	2291	768	139	10	1367	2062	2230
% enrollment	100.0%	84.3%	76.3%	73.4%	24.6%	4.5%	0.3%	43.8%	66.1%	71.5%
% dropout	0.0%	15.7%	23.7%	26.3%	31.6%	29.5%				
1986 N	3313	2842	2575	2483	802	128	10	1495	2243	2386
% enrollment	100.0%	85.8%	77.7%	74.9%	24.2%	3.9%	0.3%	45.1%	67.7%	72.0%
% dropout	0.0%	14.2%	22.3%	24.8%	30.7%	28.4%				
1987 N	3168	2764	2484	2398	723	140	10	1506	2172	2306
% enrollment	100.0%	87.2%	78.4%	75.7%	22.8%	4.4%	0.3%	47.5%	68.6%	72.8%
% dropout	0.0%	12.8%	21.6%	24.0%	29.6%	27.0%				
1988 N	3302	2849	2599	2519	731	139	12	1595	2281	2314
% enrollment	100.0%	86.3%	78.7%	76.3%	22.1%	4.2%	0.4%	48.3%	69.1%	70.1%
% dropout	0.0%	13.7%	21.3%	23.3%	29.6%	26.7%				
1989 N	2918	2510	2275	2189	657	0	19	1410	–	1410
% enrollment	100.0%	86.0%	78.0%	75.0%	22.5%	0.0%	0.7%	48.3%		48.3%
% dropout	0.0%	14.0%	22.0%	24.3%	29.2%	0.0%				
1990 N	2948	2475	2241	2165	0	0	10	–	–	10
% enrollment	100.0%	84.0%	76.0%	73.4%	0.0%	0.0%	0.3%			0.3%
% dropout	0.0%	16.0%	24.0%	26.2%	0.0%	0.0%				
1991 N	3213	2699	2431	0	0	0	–	–	–	0
% enrollment	100.0%	84.0%	75.7%	0.0%	0.0%	0.0%				0.0%
% dropout	0.0%	16.0%	24.3%	0.0%	0.0%	0.0%				
1992 N	2992	2563	0	0	0	0	–	–	–	0
% enrollment	100.0%	85.7%	0.0%	0.0%	0.0%	0.0%				0.0%
% dropout	0.0%	14.3%	0.0%	0.0%	0.0%	0.0%				

Note: Because this report is run in October against the "live" SIS+ data file,
the total graduation rate for 1988 may contain Summer 1993 graduates.

111

Appendix 6
College Selection Survey

PART ONE: GENERAL INFORMATION

INSTRUCTIONS: For each item below, please circle the number of your response or answer the question by writing your response. For example, if you are female, circle number 2 in the first question below.

1. Sex: 1. Male   2. Female

2. Home State: _____(e.g., DE, NJ MD, PA, NY, etc.)

3. a) From what type of high school did you graduate?

    1. Public   2. Private   3. Parochial

    b) State where this high school is located: _____

4. Race/Ethnic group: 1. American Indian   4. Hispanic
                             2. Asian/Pacific Islander   5. White
                             3. Black   6. Other

5. Please indicate your cumulative high school GPA:

    1. 3.5 or higher   4. 2.0 - 2.49
    2. 3.0 - 3.49   5. 1.9 or lower
    3. 2.5 - 2.99

6. Please indicate your highest set of SAT scores: SATV _____   SATM _____

7. To how many colleges or universities did you apply?

    1. One   5. Five
    2. Two   6. Six
    3. Three   7. Seven
    4. Four   8. Eight or more

8. a) To which College at the University of Delaware did you apply as your first choice?

    b) Into which College were you accepted? (Please check appropriate column.)

Apply Accept   Apply Accept
___   ___   1. Agricultural Sci.   ___   ___   5. Education
___   ___   2. Arts & Science (except   ___   ___   6. Engineering
                undeclared)   ___   ___   7. Human Resources
___   ___   3. Arts & Science, undeclared   ___   ___   8. Nursing
___   ___   4. Business & Economics   ___   ___   9. Physical Education

113

PART TWO: COLLEGE SELECTION

1. Please list **in order of preference** the three colleges or universities that were at the top of your application list. Then answer the two questions to the right.

	Were you accepted?		Were you awarded any financial aid?		
	Yes	No	Yes	No	Did not Apply for aid
1st Choice: _____	1	2	1	2	3
2nd Choice: _____	1	2	1	2	3
3rd Choice: _____	1	2	1	2	3

2. Was the financial aid package you received the decisive factor in your final selection of a college?

      1. Yes   2. No   3. Not applicable

3. If you received a financial aid award, was a scholarship based strictly on academic merit a part of your aid package:

  a) at the University of Delaware?   1. Yes   2. No

  b) at other college(s)?   1. Yes   2. No

4. During the college choice process, did your preference for the University of Delaware change?

      1. Yes, moved up
      2. Yes, moved down
      3. Did not change

5. Which of the following statements best characterizes your college enrollment decision?

      1. I am enrolling at the University of Delaware.
      2. I am enrolling at another college.
          Please specify the name of that college:
          _____
      3. I am uncertain where I will be enrolling.
      4. I am not enrolling at any college at this time.

114

PART THREE: COLLEGE-UNIVERSITY CHARACTERISTICS

We want to learn about how you view the characteristics of the University of Delaware in comparison to other colleges and universities to which you have applied, been accepted, and seriously considered attending. Please complete this section by first indicating how important the characteristic was in influencing your enrollment decision (circle the most appropriate response). If you are attending Delaware next fall, indicate how you rate the various characteristics at both the University of Delaware and the school you would have not decided to enroll at Delaware. Be sure to write the name of the school you would have attended in the blank provided. If you are attending a different college, indicate how Delaware compares to the school you will be attending. Again, be sure to include the name of the school you will be attending. If you do not know enough about an item, please indicate "don't know" (circle number 5).

How Important Is this To You?			Characteristic	University of Delaware					School You Would Have or Will Attend Name: _____				
Very Important	Somewhat Important	Not Important		Very Good	Good	Poor	Very Poor	Don't Know	Very Good	Good	Poor	Very Poor	Don't Know
1	2	3	1. Quality of academics	1	2	3	4	5	1	2	3	4	5
1	2	3	2. Honors Program	1	2	3	4	5	1	2	3	4	5
1	2	3	3. Personal attention given to students by faculty	1	2	3	4	5	1	2	3	4	5
1	2	3	4. General reputation of university	1	2	3	4	5	1	2	3	4	5
1	2	3	5. Quality of faculty	1	2	3	4	5	1	2	3	4	5
1	2	3	6. Total cost (tuition, fees, room & board)	1	2	3	4	5	1	2	3	4	5
1	2	3	7. Social activities	1	2	3	4	5	1	2	3	4	5
1	2	3	8. Financial aid package	1	2	3	4	5	1	2	3	4	5
1	2	3	9. Closeness to home	1	2	3	4	5	1	2	3	4	5
1	2	3	10. Size of enrollment	1	2	3	4	5	1	2	3	4	5
1	2	3	11. Quality of programs in your intended major	1	2	3	4	5	1	2	3	4	5
1	2	3	12. Diversity of student body	1	2	3	4	5	1	2	3	4	5
1	2	3	13. Housing opportunities	1	2	3	4	5	1	2	3	4	5
1	2	3	14. Intercollegiate athletic program	1	2	3	4	5	1	2	3	4	5
1	2	3	15. Athletic facilities	1	2	3	4	5	1	2	3	4	5
1	2	3	16. Faculty teaching reputation	1	2	3	4	5	1	2	3	4	5
1	2	3	17. Overall treatment as prospective students	1	2	3	4	5	1	2	3	4	5
1	2	3	18. Promptness of replies to requests for information	1	2	3	4	5	1	2	3	4	5

Of the characteristics above, which three factors (in order of importance) most influenced your enrollment decision?

Most important factor: # _____   Second most important: # _____   Third most important: # _____

PART FOUR: INFORMATION SOURCES

We are interested in learning which sources of information students use to learn about the University of Delaware, whether the information provided by the source was positive or negative, and how important that source and information was in shaping your choice of a college. For each of the information sources **that you actually used**, please indicate whether the information you received about the University was positive or negative. Also, for those sources you used, indicate how important that information was to you in your selection of a college. Circle the number corresponding to you choice.

INFORMATION SOURCE	IMPACT						IMPORTANCE		
	Didn't use this Source	Very Positive	Positive	No Impact	Negative	Very Negative	Very Important	Somewhat Important	Not Important
1. Viewbook	1	2	3	4	5	6	1	2	3
2. Campus Visit	1	2	3	4	5	6	1	2	3
3. College Comparison Guides (e.g., Peterson's, Barron's)	1	2	3	4	5	6	1	2	3
4. Parents	1	2	3	4	5	6	1	2	3
5. Friends	1	2	3	4	5	6	1	2	3
6. Current students at UD	1	2	3	4	5	6	1	2	3
7. High school teacher	1	2	3	4	5	6	1	2	3
8. High school guidance counselor	1	2	3	4	5	6	1	2	3
9. Alumnus of the University	1	2	3	4	5	6	1	2	3
10. Mailing from the Honors Program	1	2	3	4	5	6	1	2	3
11. High school visit by an admissions officer	1	2	3	4	5	6	1	2	3
12. Athletic staff	1	2	3	4	5	6	1	2	3
13. Home/hotel receptions	1	2	3	4	5	6	1	2	3

List in order of importance (by selecting from the numbers 1-13 above) the three most important influences on your decision as to which college to attend:

Most important influence: # _____   Second most important: # _____   Third most important: # _____

Thank you for your cooperation

Appendix 7
Career Plans Survey

| Name : | If any of this information is incorrect |
| Address : | use the space below to change it: |

SSN :
Degree :   Degree Received :
Major :

Please write the number that corresponds to your answer in the box(es) to the left of each question.

EMPLOYMENT STATUS

1. Please select the item which best describes your current employment status:
   1. I hold or have accepted a full-time job related to my major.
   2. I hold or have accepted a full-time job unrelated to my major.
   3. I hold or have accepted a part-time job related to my major.
   4. I hold or have accepted a part-time job unrelated to my major.
   5. I am in or am about to enter the military.
   6. I am not seeking a job, because I am continuing my education.
   7. I am not pursuing a job at this time.
   8. I am actively seeking employment at this time.

2. If you are actively seeking employment, do you desire assistance from the Career Planning and Placement Office?
   1. Yes   2. No

3. If you are employed, which item best describes your position? (If you are not employed, go to question 9.)
   1. It is my first career position.
   2. It is a position which I have held for over a year.
   3. It is a temporary position, unrelated to my career.

4. What is your JOB TITLE? (Please print in the boxes below)

Name of Employer: (Please print below)

Address of Employer: _____

5. If you are in a teaching position, which item best describes your contractual arrangement?
   1. Full-time contract
   2. Long-term/permanent substitute
   3. Per diem (daily) substitute
   4. Other: _____

6. Please indicate the geographic area in which you will be working:

01. New Castle County, DE	07. New York	12. South
02. Kent County, DE	08. Virginia	13. South-West
03. Sussex County, DE	09. West Virginia	14. Mid-West
04. Pennsylvania	10. Washington, D. C.	15. West
05. Maryland	11. New England States	16. Outside continental U.S.A.
06. New Jersey		

118

7. What method(s) were most important in obtaining this position? (You may select up to 4 methods.)
   01. Heard about the position from a friend/family member
   02. Advertisement in a newspaper or magazine
   03. Academic department notice or faculty referral
   04. Private employment service
   05. Internship/cooperative with present employer
   06. Job listing in Career Planning Office (or Job Vacancy Bulletin)
   07. Campus Interview Program
   08. Research in Career Resource Center
   09. College Career Day (Nursing Career Day, Project Search, etc.)
   10. Previously employed by present employer
   11. Other _____

8. Please indicate your current annual salary. Salary information is important in advising students about various careers. Individual salaries are strictly confidential and will be reported only as group averages.

9. Please put the number 1 in the box by each of the Career Planning and Placement Office services you utilized as a student:
   1. Campus Interview Program   5. Credentials Service
   2. Career planning workshops   6. Individual counseling
   3. Career Resource Center   7. Job listing service
   4. Internship Program   8. Other _____
                                            (please specify)

EDUCATIONAL PLANS

10. Which of the following corresponds to your educational plans at this time:
    1. Going to graduate or professional school full-time with financial aid in the form of a fellowship or assistantship
    2. Going to graduate or professsional school full-time at my own expense
    3. Going to graduate or professional school part-time
    4. Not pursuing further formal education

11. If you have been accepted by a graduate or professional school or are currently attending a school, please indicate the name of the school:

12. What is your major field of study in graduate or professional school?
    01. Agricultural Sciences
    02. Architecture
    03. Art
    04. Biological Sciences
    05. Business or Economics
    06. Dentistry
    07. Education (including Physical Education)
    08. Engineering
    09. Humanities (English, Languages, Philosophy, etc.)
    10. Law
    11. Library Science
    12. Mathematics (including Statistics & Computer Science)
    13. Medicine
    14. Nursing
    15. Performing Arts or Music
    16. Physical Sciences (Chemistry, Physics, Geology, etc.)
    17. Social Sciences (Anthropology, Geography, Political Science, Psychology, Sociology, etc.)
    18. Veterinary Medicine
    19. Other (please specify) _____

13. What type of degree program are you taking?
    1. Master's degree (M.A., M.B.A., M.F.A.)
    2. Academic Doctorate (Ph.D. or Ed.D.)
    3. Professional degree (e.g., MD, LLB, DVM, DDS, JD, etc.)
    4. Non-degree certificate program (e.g., paralegal, dietetics, etc.)

Thank you for participating

119

Appendix 8
Salaried Staff Interest Survey

Salaried Staff Interest Survey

The Salaried Staff Constituent Group of the Commission on the Status of Women is conducting a survey aimed at obtaining information that will assist the CSW in identifying issues of importance to salaried staff members. PLEASE RETURN THE COMPLETED QUESTIONNAIRE TO THE OFFICE OF WOMEN'S AFFAIRS, 303 HULLIHEN HALL, BY MONDAY, DECEMBER 21, 1992. Call the Office of Women's Affairs at 831-8063 if you have questions.

(For Office Use Only)

☐

1. Please check one:
    ____ Female   ____ Male

☐

2. How long have you been employed at the University?
    ____ 1 to 3 years   ____ 5 to 10 years
    ____ 3 to 5 years   ____ over 10 years

☐

3. What is your job classification?
    ____ Library Family   ____ Service Family
    ____ Records Family   ____ Technical Family
    ____ Secretarial Family

4. Please rate the following issues using this scale:
    1) MOST Important
    2) Very Important
    3) Somewhat Important
    4) Not Very Important
    5) LEAST Important

☐
☐
☐
☐

Family/Work Issues:
    ____ Dependent/Sick Care
    ____ University Sponsored On-Site Child Care
    ____ Flexible Working Hours
    ____ Current State Pension Retirement Benefits

University Issues:

☐
☐
☐
☐
☐

    ____ Campus Safety
    ____ Being required by supervisor to perform personal tasks at work
    ____ Being required to perform additonal tasks (due to downsizing) that are not part of your job description
    ____ Harassment (sexual or other)
    ____ Other (please specify): _____

Any comments you wish to express: _____
_____
_____
_____

Thank you for your help!

121

Index

Accreditation 14-15
Ad Hoc Requests 36
AIR Forum 16-17
Assessment
    of Faculty and Staff 61-62
    of Institutions 60-61
    of Students 48-60
    Overview 44-48
    Portfolio 57

Computer Software 20-23
    Spreadsheets 21-22
    Statistical 21-22
    Word Processing and Desktop Publishing 22

Data Sharing 29
    Consortia 29
    National Cooperative Data Share (NCDS) 28-29
Data Sources
    Commercial 26
    External 27-30
    Internal 32
Data Collection 34-35
    Standard Production Reports 35-36

Electronic Communication 23-26
    Bitnet 24-26
    E-mail 24
    Internet 24-26
Enrollment Management
    Admissions Marketing 37, 41-42
    Admissions Recruitment 37
    Financial Aid 39
    Retention 40-41

Finances
    Current Funds Revenues and Expenditures 68-73
    Education and General Revenues and Expenditures 68-73
    Interinstitutional Financial Data 73-74

Ratio Analysis 70
State Appropriations 70
Fiscal/Economic Considerations 6

Government/Regulatory Considerations 7

I-P-O Model 1-11
Implementation Strategies 91-95
Institutional Mission 1, 5, 36, 59
Institutional Research Resources
    AIR Professional File 16
    Books 12-16
    Computing 18-23
    Electronic Communication 23-76
    Journals 12-16
    Monographs 12-16
    Professional Associations 16-18
Institutional Research, Definition of 1
Integrated Postsecondary Education Data
    System (IPEDS) 19, 27-28, 58, 73, 75

Marketplace Considerations 7

National Data Service for Higher Education 28-29

Peer Comparators 41-42, 73-74
Productivity
    Administrative 70
    Instructional 84-88
    Interinstitutional Comparisons 73-74, 89-90
    Research and Service 88-89
Professional Associations 13-15

Retention Rates 40-41

Salary
    Comparisons 76
    Equity 78
Self-Study 14
Students
    Assessment of 48-60
    Retention 40

as Systems Component 9
Surveys
    Admitted Student Questionnaire 50-52
    Annual Survey of Colleges 28
    Campus Community Scale 61
    College Selection Survey 52-53
    College Student Experiences Survey 54-56
    Commercial 30
    Exit 57
    Faculty Quality of Life 62
    Integrated Postsecondary Education Data
        System (IPEDS) 19, 27-28, 58, 73, 75
    Locally Prepared 30-32
    NCDS 28-29
    New Student Orientation 60-61
    Student Information Form 50
    Student Needs Survey 56
    Student Opinion Survey 53-54
    SUNY Albany 56

Total Quality Management 15